# ANDY

Andy sat in the old and torn armchair, the light green material faded with age and use. There are several armchairs against the wall and three coffee tables with magazines and newspapers discarded on them. The walls are painted light grey having recently been redecorated, and the false ceiling with hash blinding lights. The flooring, half with dark grey carpet, worn and torn at the centre, the rest exposing the old green tiles, cracked, worn, and polished. Opposite the seating area is a kitchen, on one side two large refrigerators with various fridge magnets, and a collection of different vacations and trips. A white worktop runs the length of the room, with a sink and draining board at the centre—cupboards above and below. The draining board has over twenty mugs on it, several balanced on the top. There are two large windows, both blocked with a breezeblock wall, light barely getting in at the sides.
The door opened and Jeff, one of the porters looked at Andy.

"Andy!" He yelped.

Andy jumped in fright, forcing a smile.

Jeff is the same height as Andy, slim with long greying hair and a messy, thick beard. His arms are plastered with various bad tattoos, a selection of snakes and insects.

"What you doing?" He said.

"Waiting on Brian," Andy said. "Finished the washing up."

"Brian asked me to give you some work," Jeff said thinking. "Not sure what we can give you, but are you open to doing anything?" Jeff asked curiously.

"Yes," Andy said. "Anything to keep me busy."

"Toilets need cleaning," Jeff said.

"What?" Andy said bluntly.

"Did you not hear me?" Jeff laughed. "I said the toilets need doing."

"Yes I heard you," Andy said. "Thought you were taking the piss."

"No," Jeff said. "I can show you where the cleaning stuff is and the brushes," He scoffed. "You are gonna need brushes, some of the shit has dried on!" He laughed. "I think Brian left behind a torpedo in one of the stalls."

Andy groaned in disgust.

"It's not that bad!" Jeff exclaimed. "It's only poo!"

"Do the porters do the cleaning then?" Andy asked.

"No," Jeff said. "We don't do stuff like that!"

"So why are you asking me to clean the toilets?" Andy asked. "If it isn't part of the role?"

"Brian doesn't want you on the grounds for a couple of days," Jeff said. "I think he is annoyed with you."

"Why?" Andy asked. "It is literally my first day."

"You were late," Jeff said. "Brian is fussy like that."

"I was sent to the main reception," Andy said. "I have the letter and everything."

"Oh right," Jeff said.

"It's no fun being blamed for something that was out of my control," Andy said, annoyance in his voice.

"Yeah, well?" Jeff said, stuttering. "Cleaning stuff is under the sink," He pointed. "You need training?"

"Do I need training?" Andy asked. "On how to clean a toilet?"

"Yeah?" Jeff nodded.

"I think I will manage," Andy bluntly responded. "Not rocket science is it?"

"Good stuff!" Jeff held up his thumbs. "I am off to have a fag break, see you later!"

Jeff left in a hurry, Andy sat back in the chair, and his hands went to his face as he groaned.

"No way," Andy said softly. "I am not cleaning the toilets!"

The door opened and Andy looked up, expecting to see Jeff but Eileen stood there, staring at Andy, holding a brown envelope.

"Andy?" She asked.

"Yes?" Andy said.

"I am Eileen," She said. "I run dispatch and look after the portering team."

Eileen is a large woman, of average height with a light blue summer dress, black heels, and a large red plastic necklace. Her long blonde hair was curly and messy. She is wearing red glasses, the bright frames emphasizing the red lipstick she has on.

"I am Eileen," She said. "Are you the deaf lad on work experience?" She forced a smile.

"I am Andy yes," Andy said.

She handed the envelope to Andy, who smiled as he took it and looked inside, removing an identification badge and a lanyard.

"I've been told to ask for a twenty pounds deposit," She said, holding out her hand.

"Don't have any money on me," Andy said.

She took the identification from him, snatching the envelope.

"Then bring it in tomorrow," She snapped.

"Actually," Andy said. "I won't be back tomorrow," He said.

"Why?" She asked.

"I have been here a few hours and been made very unwelcome," Andy said. "All I have done is made tea and coffee, washed up and now I am expected to clean the toilets!" Andy moaned.

"Well you have to start somewhere," She said. "That is life."

"But nothing I have done today is part of the role," Andy said.

"That is true," She said. "But call it experience, it must be so hard for a disabled person such as yourself to find a job, so you cannot be picky."

"No," Andy stood up. "Not wasting my time with this crap."

"What do you mean?" Eileen asked. "I am confused."

"I am not staying," Andy said. "I am leaving."

"You cannot leave," She said. "You will not get paid!"

"It's work experience," Andy scoffed. "They are not paying me!"

Eileen looked at Andy in confusion.

"It's raining out, maybe you should wait for Brian," She stuttered.

"I am going," Andy said.

6

"You will get wet!" She exclaimed.

"You might melt in the rain, but I will be fine," Andy grinned. "I am not scrubbing shit-covered toilets and being a tea maid."

"Brian will be upset!" She said. "He is looking forward to working with you."

"Oh bollocks is he," Andy said. "He will have to make his own drinks!"

Andy walked away, looking back at Eileen before leaving, closing the door behind him.

Andy looked up at the flickering light, yawning as he rested his head against the wall. The rain battered against the windows in front of him, so heavy it blurred the outside world. He sat at the table in the portable cabin room where there were four rows of two desks, with a desktop computer at the middle of each desk. On one side of the cabin, separated by large notice boards, are various posters. Against the walls, covering two large windows are cabinets missing the doors, the shelves loaded with papers, books, and stationery. In the far corner are two desks with more modern computers on them. At the end, a door leading outside, slightly ajar, a small puddle forming on the mat. In front of the desks, is a large dry wipe board, and at the end of it an emergency door leading to an alleyway behind the church.

Andy is seventeen years old, short, and slim with wet dark blonde hair. He is wearing a damp white shirt with the sleeves rolled up, black trousers and black polished shoes.

The door opened and a girl walked in, tall and slim with long blonde hair, wearing blue jeans and a white t-shirt. She walked up behind Any, shoving him playfully.

Andy yelped and turned around, smiling when he saw the girl.

"What are you doing?" He said. "You scared me!"

"You are in trouble!" The girl said, smacking her hand in mock. "Just saw Miss Fleet." The girl is profoundly deaf, her voice slightly impaired and more nasal. She also signs some of what she speaks.

"Oh?" Andy said. "Why?"

"Your work experience," She said. "The hospital is very angry with you."

"Oh right," Andy said. "It was shit."

"Why?" She said.

"Because it was," Andy said. "Treating me like I was stupid because I am deaf."

"Bad boy," The girl laughed. "Always drama!" She moaned. "Always drama with you!" She poked him in the chest.

"No not me," Andy said. "Why are you not at yours?"

"Sick," She said. "So was not allowed."

"Poor you," Andy said imitating a violin. "All those crisps you eat!"

"Shut up!" She punched him in the arm.

"Feeling better?" Andy asked.

She nodded.

"Why are you wet?" She said in disgust. "You wet yourself again?"

"Very funny!" Andy rolled his eyes.

"Want to go for a walk after school?" She asked. "Seafront?"

"Sure," Andy said. "Who is going?"

"Few of us," She said. "Going to Rottingdean first for burger."

"I am up for that," Andy said.

"Got to go," She said. "Hope you get smacked bum!"

The girl laughed and ran out of the room, pulling the door closed but it opened again.

Andy walked to the window, looking outside for a few minutes, unaware of the woman who walked into the portable cabin behind him.

"Andy?" She said, annoyance in her voice.

Andy didn't respond and continued to look outside.

"Andy?!" The woman said louder, stomping on the floor.

The woman, tall and slim, is wearing a dark blue blouse and black trousers. Her heels are light blue and metallic. She holds a notepad in one hand and the other a black mug.

Andy turned around in fright.

"Is your hearing aid on?" She asked curiously, putting down the pad and coffee on the desk at the end of the room, pointing to her ear.

"No," Andy said, removing a hearing aid from his pocket. "Hold on," He said putting it into his left ear, looking upwards as he switched it on. "One two three, hello, hello!" He said. "Yes, it is on now."

"Sit down please," She said pointing to the chair next to her.

Andy sat down, covering his mouth as he yawned.

"Why are you wet?" She asked, sitting down, and opening her notebook.

"Got caught in the rain," Andy said. "Walked back from town."

"Why didn't you get the bus?" She asked curiously. "Or the school minibus?"

"Couldn't be bothered," Andy said. "Was a nice walk back."

"Well don't complain when you catch a cold," She rolled her eyes.

"I don't get colds," Andy said smugly.

"Famous last words," The woman crossed her legs. "I just had a rather angry phone call," She sighed. "Can you guess who from?"

"The hospital?" Andy said. "I am surprised he noticed I was gone."

"Yes," She shook her head. "They said you came in late and then walked out without saying anything."

"I was late because I was told to go to reception," Andy said. "They said that I should have gone to the portering office, but no one said that to me."

"I was told you had to report to the reception," The woman said. "That is their fault, not yours," She wrote down some notes. "So why did you leave?"

"The manager was pretty rude," Andy said. "When I couldn't understand him, he told me to try harder to listen."

"Oh dear," She said. "That isn't very nice."

"I am sorry Miss Fleet," Andy said. "But it was horrible."

"So what happened?" Miss Fleet said. "Why did you walk out?"

"The manager said he didn't want me working in public and said the best thing I could do was make tea and coffee for the porters," Andy scoffed. "I did fifteen cups of tea and coffee and then was asked to clean the porter's kitchen and wash up."

"Did you?" Miss Fleet asked.

"No," Andy said. "He wanted me to clean the toilets after," Andy cringed. "Trust me, if you had seen them!"

"Okay," Miss Fleet nodded. "I will discuss this with him, but he is very angry and said he isn't impressed."

"Sorry, but what is the point of work experience if I am not going to do portering?" Andy said.

"What happened with the computer place?" Miss Fleet said. "Did you enjoy that?"

"Yes," Andy nodded. "I wanted a change."

"What about the film production office?" She said, flicking through the notes.

"I was there for three days, and every day they wanted me to organise the tapes," Andy said. "One day in alphabetical order, then numerical order and then date order."

"You have to start somewhere," She chuckled. "Even if it is boring."

"Anything in performing arts?" Andy said. "What about the theatres?"

"The best they could offer was the front desk," Miss Fleet said. "And that requires answering the telephone."

"What about the video store?" Andy said. "I would be cool with that."

"They are not accepting anyone for work experience," She said. "Besides you would be watching horror films all day."

"What is wrong with that?" Andy laughed.

"Well, you are not eighteen for one!" Miss Fleet said. "So, what do we do with you?"

"I don't know," Andy shrugged his shoulders. "Cinema?"

"No," she laughed. "It's work experience for a reason, not watch films all day."

Andy sighed in frustration, looking around the room.

"How do you feel about working for an undertaker?" Miss Fleet asked curiously. "My partner used to be an undertaker, might be perfect for you."

"Now that sounds interesting," Andy said. "Very."

"You will need to take it seriously," She warned him. "I know you love all the death and gore, but you will need to tone it down, especially at a Funeral Directors."

"I can tone it down," Andy smiled.

"My lessons would say otherwise," She rolled her eyes. "The comments you drop go over people's heads."

"Deaf people don't have a sense of humour," Andy scoffed.

"Not everyone has your kind of sense of humour," Miss Fleet said. "And then there is the language barrier."

"I guess," Andy said.

"I will look up some local Funeral Directors," Miss Fleet said. "And see if we can get something organised for next week."

"Sounds good," Andy nodded.

"Otherwise," Miss Fleet looked at Andy. "You will be doing a week of work experience in the school!"

"Pass!" Andy groaned.

"Don't let me down," Miss Fleet said warning him.

"I won't," Andy said giving her a thumbs up.

"So what are you doing for the rest of the day?" Miss Fleet said looking at the clock. "Have you had lunch?"

"No," Andy said. "I was going to do some writing, in here if that is okay?"

"I have a class after lunch," Miss Fleet said. "But you can use the computers round the side, but no interruptions please."

"Thanks," Andy said. "Can I get permission to go to the dorm and get changed?"

"Yes," Miss Fleet said. "But let Terry know, he is in the staff room."

"Okay," Andy said. "Thank you."

Andy let the portable cabin, running through the rain towards the dorms on the other side of the school grounds.

Andy knocked on the door, stepped back and waited. The small hall, leading from the front door has a door directly ahead, the staff dorm room where the house parent would stay overnight. On the left a door leading to the living area and kitchen, and on the right stairs leading upstairs.

The door opened and Terry, tall and athletically built with shoulder-length dark brown hair and stubble.

"Andy," he said. "I heard you were on site."

"Yeah," Andy said. "Miss Fleet said it was okay to get changed, but to check in with you first."

"Did you walk back in the rain?" Terry said smiling. "It's refreshing isn't it?"

"It was yes," Andy said.

"What happened?" Terry said. "With the work experience?"

"It was crap," Andy scoffed. "They had me making the tea and coffee, washing up and then wanted me to clean the toilets!"

"Do the other porters do that?" Terry said. "The cleaning of toilets?"

"Not as far as I know," Andy said. "The manager also had an issue with me being deaf, so it was for the best I didn't stay."

"Are you okay?" Terry said. "Need to talk about it or?"

"I am okay," Andy said. "Miss Fleet is going to try and get me a placement with the undertakers in town."

"Really?" Terry said, slightly confused. "You up for that?"

Andy nodded.

"Fair enough," Terry nodded in appreciation. "I am impressed. Anyhow, go and put some dry clothes on and then get lunch, let me know before you leave."

"Will do, thanks Terry," Andy said and turned to make his way upstairs.

"Hold on Andy," Terry said. "Are you having issues with Ahmet still?"

"What?" Andy said with worry.

"Ahmet," He said. "Is he still giving you problems?"

"Not really," Andy said. "Not so much since I moved rooms."

"Are you sure?" Terry asked. "I won't tolerate his bullying, and I know it still happens."

"I will tell you if anything happens," Andy said. "Maybe he got bored of making my life a misery."

Terry sighed heavily.

"Clare told me about last week," Terry shook his head. "When Ahmet got his pillow, wet with urine and rubbed it on your face and tried to smother you."

"Yeah that wasn't fun," Andy said. "Clare had words with him I think."

"The little shit needs a clout," Terry said. "Just because he thinks he is untouchable."

"Karma will pay him a visit one day," Andy said. "I am sure of it."

"Let me know when you are ready," Terry said looking at his watch. "I will join you for lunch, I am starved."

# MONDAY

Andy walked up to the door, looking through the window into the Funeral Showroom, trying to look through the gap in the blinds, the harsh sunlight reflecting off the tinted windows.

He is wearing black trousers, a white shirt, a black tie, and polished black shoes. He has hearing aids in both ears, and his dark blonde hair is short at the back and sides, spikey on top. A silver watch on his left wrist, the strap in tanned leather.

He tried the door, an aluminium frame with a glass inner, realising it was locked and then knocked on the glass.

"Anyone in?" He said looking through the glass. "Hello?"

Looking to his right, he noticed an intercom.

"Oh," He said. "This will be fun."

He pressed the button on the intercom, bending down so his ear was closer to the speaker, listening to the prolonged buzz.

"Yes?" A woman's voice came over. "How can I help you?"

"Hi," Andy said. "Sorry, but I cannot hear very well."

"Hello, can I help you?" The woman asked again.

"Sorry but I cannot hear," Andy said. "I am deaf," he groaned when a lorry drove slowly past, the breaks squealing as it slowed down.

"What do you need?" She asked.

"What?" Andy said. "Can you repeat that?"

"We are not open until nine," She said. "Could you come back please?"

"I am working here this week," Andy said loudly. "I am a student on work experience."

"Who are you?" She asked.

"What?" Andy said.

"Wait a moment," The woman said.

"Sorry I cannot hear," Andy said. "Not a single word!"

"Wait a moment!" The woman said louder.

"Hello?" Andy said getting closer to the speaker.

A minute passed and Andy scoffed, yawning loudly, and looking around. He glanced at his watch, muttering to himself.

"Serves my right for getting in early," he said.

Andy pressed the intercom again.

"Yes?" The woman's voice again.

"I am still here," Andy said. "Could someone let me in?"

"Who are you?" The woman asked.

"I am deaf," Andy said.

"Deaf who?" The woman said, slightly annoyed.

Andy looked around in frustration, noticing a postman walking down the path towards him.

"Excuse me?" Andy said. "Could you help?"

The postman is wearing a red t-shirt, grey shorts, and brown hiking boots. He has long hair and a messy beard.

"Sure," He said curiously. "What's up?" He said.

"Could you speak to the woman on the end for me?" Andy said. "I am deaf and cannot hear on the intercom."

"Sure mate," The postman said. "Is it on?"

"Who is this please?" The woman said on the intercom.

"Hi," The postman said. "There is a young guy here," He said. "What's your name?"

"Andy," Andy replied.

"Said his name is Andy and he is deaf," The postman said.

"I am here on work experience," Andy added.

"Said he is doing work experience here," He looked up at the signage and then back at Andy. "Work Experience," He scoffed. "Really?"

"Yeah," Andy said.

"Morbid little git!" The postman cringed.

"Who are you calling little?" Andy asked.

"Oh, my God!" The girl said. "I am so sorry, I am coming down now."

"She is coming down," The postman said. "Here, give her this," He said, handing Andy a pack of letters held together with an elastic band.

"Sure," Andy said nodding.

"Have fun," The postman shook his head. "Morbid!" He laughed as he walked away, shaking his head.

A few minutes passed and the door clicked, Andy turned around to find Leanne standing there holding the door open, short, and slim

18

with long brown hair and glasses. She is wearing black trousers and a white blouse.

"I am so sorry," She said. "I had no idea that you are deaf."

"It's fine," Andy said handing the pack of letters to her.

"Andy is it?" She said. "You are early."

"Shall I come back?" Andy said looking at his watch?"

"No," Leanne said and smiled. "You can come in a wait if you want, Martin is running late."

"If that is okay?" Andy said.

"Yes, that is fine," She said, moving to the side. "You can have a look around if you want."

"Thanks," Andy nodded, letting himself in, awkwardly standing at the side.

"Tea or Coffee?" She asked, closing the door, and locking it.

"No thanks," Andy said. "Just had breakfast."

"Lucky you!" She said. "Take a seat, hopefully, Martin won't be long," She said pointing at the two-seater couch.

"Thanks," Andy said and sat on the edge of the two-seater couch facing the full-length window looking out into the high street.

"Didn't realise you were hard of hearing," She said pointing to his ears.

She turned, looking at the blinds.

"Just a moment," She said and walked over to them, pulling the cord, and looking up at the runners as the blinds slowly opened, rattling against the window. "I always forget these," She laughed.

"I am severely deaf," Andy said as she walked back towards to couch. "Hard to hear intercoms on a busy street."

"I was quite loud," She said.

"Not as loud as the lorry that drove past," Andy scoffed. "I get overwhelmed easily with noise."

"Sorry about that," She said. "I have never met a deaf person before."

"It's nothing special," Andy smiled. "Just like any other normal person, just with a lot more ignoring."

"That is funny," Leanne laughed. "I need to get back to it," She said pointing upstairs and hurried to a door at the end of the room, opening it and then closing it behind her.

"Sure," Andy said nodding.

On either side of the large room are various designs of coffins, three mounted on the wall perfectly in line with each other. A display cabinet with urns, plagues and bibles is at the centre of the room. The blood red carpet is clean, the walls in magnolia and the ceilings pure white, the warm glow from the three-bulb lighting at the centre. Behind the couch are two doors, one leading to a waiting room, and another leading to a hall to the rest of the building. On both sides of the doors, are large golden framed mirrors, clean and polished.

Andy picked up a local paper, flipping through it and occasionally looking up at the window. After a few minutes, he noticed a polished black hearse parked up at the front.

A bell rang as the front door opened and Andy jumped, looking up and straightening his tie.

20

Arthur walked in slowly, a man in his sixties, tall and slim with a thin grey beard, his grey hair short on the back and sides, long on top.

"Windy out there!" He said trying to tidy his hair with his fingers.

"Sorry?" Andy said.

"What for?" Arthur replied.

"What?" Andy said in confusion.

"You said sorry," Arthur said. "Now I am confused," Arthur chuckled. "I said it's windy out," He raised his voice slightly.

"Didn't hear what you said," Andy smiled. "I am deaf."

"Ah, you must be Andy!" Arthur said and walked over, holding out his hand. "Martin mentioned that you would be spending some time with us."

"Nice to meet you," Andy said shaking Arthur's hand.

"I am Arthur," He smiled. "Call me Art," He said. "Arthur makes me feel old."

"Will do," Andy nodded.

"How long are you with us?" Art asked.

"A week," Andy said.

"Still at school?" Art asked curiously.

"Yes," Andy said. "Work experience to top it off."

"I am curious," Art said. "What made you pick the funeral business? Surely there are plenty of more exciting options?"

"Are there?" Andy said curiously.

"Well, kids nowadays like computers?" Art said. "Or something a little less," He looked around and held up his hands. "This."

"It has never been done before," Andy said. "I wanted to do something different."

"Done anything like this before?" Art said.

"No," Andy said.

"Squeamish?" Art grinned.

"Not a chance," Andy said. "Grew up with horror." Arthur nodded.

"It's quite different to the movies," Art said. "Not as bad as people think."

"I am looking forward to it," Andy said.

"How old are you if you don't mind me asking?" Art asked Andy.

"Seventeen," Andy said. "How about you?"

"Have a guess," Art said and smiled.

"Late fifties?" Andy said, shrugging his shoulders. "I am terrible with ages."

"Sixty-five," Art said. "Today, but don't tell everyone, don't want to have to share the cake!"

"Won't say a thing!" Andy laughed.

"Been here long?" Art looked at his watch. "Wasn't expecting you here until nine."

"Thought I would make an effort and get in early," Andy said. "Got here quicker than I planned."

"Show off," Art scoffed. "Does Martin know if you are in?" Art said and looked at his watch. "Scrap that," He laughed. "Martin won't be here yet."

"A lady came down," Andy said. "I never caught her name."

22

"Young?" Art asked.

Andy nodded.

"Leanne," Art said. "She hasn't been with us long."

"Seems quite friendly," Andy said.

"She is," Art said. "She is brilliant on the sales side, amazing with people."

"How long have you been here?" Andy asked.

"Do you mean with the company?" Art said. "Fifteen years or so."

"Oh cool," Andy said.

"Had my own business before that," Art said. "After my wife died, I wanted a change, and here I am."

"Sorry to hear that," Andy said.

"It's okay," Art smiled. "She was very unwell, it was good for her to go."

"Okay," Andy said.

"Any idea who you are working with today?" Art said.

"No," Andy said. "I was told to meet Martin and I would shadow him."

"Have you met him yet?" Art said with a grin.

"No," Andy said. "I only met the manager upstairs, last week."

"Woman with the silver hair?" Art chuckled. "That is Marcia, did she scare you?"

Andy laughed, shaking his head.

"A little," Andy said. "She reminded me of a school headmistress."

"She scares the crap out of everyone here," Art said. "She is the wife of the owner, whatever you do, don't swear around her."

"I don't swear," Andy said.

"Really," Art said, not quite believing him.

"Really," Andy nodded with a grin. "I don't swear."

"Not sure I believe you," Art said.

"It's true," Andy said. "I am talking bollocks!" He whispered.

The bell rang and the door opened.

"And here he is," Art said. "Are you ever going to get in on time?"

Martin smiled sarcastically and shook his head. He is tall and heavily built with a shaved head and a thick trimmed beard. Wearing a black suit, white shirt, black tie, and a blood-red waistcoat. He has a silver coffee flask in one hand and in the other, a black briefcase.

"Who is this?" He indicated towards Andy.

"Andy," Art said. "Working with us for the week, work experience."

"Oh bollocks," Martin said. "I thought that was next week!"

"Guess he isn't scared of Marcia?" Andy laughed.

"What's that?" Martin asked with a smile.

"Told him about Marcia and her dislike of swearing," Art laughed.

"I wouldn't worry about it down here," Martin said. "She never comes down here, so, bollocks!"

Andy laughed.

"You should see the swear jar they have upstairs," Art said. "They use it for cakes every other week."

"That's why we are all fat," Martin scoffed.

"We?" Art said, looking Martin up and down.

"Behave!" Martin scoffed. "You are keen," Martin said, looking at his watch and then walking over to Andy, putting his case under his arm, and holding out his hand. "What time were you told to come in?"

Andy took his hand, shaking it.

"Nine," Andy said. "Thought I would get in early."

"If I had known," Art said. "He could have helped me with the hearse."

"What time did you get in then?" Martin scoffed. "Don't you have a life?"

"Six," Art said. "Sorted out a few things for the morning."

"Great," Martin said. "Might get Andy here to shadow Gerald this morning," Martin said. "What do you think?"

"Sounds good," Art said. "I am more than happy to help out."

"What do you fancy doing?" Martin asked Andy.

"I really don't mind," Andy said.

"What about the obvious?" Art said indicating to the door at the end of the room.

"Oh yes," Martin nodded in agreement. "Have you seen a body before Andy?" Martin asked.

"Depends," Andy said.

"Depends on what?" Art asked.

"On if anyone looks under my grandmother's patio," Andy smiled. "Or my aunts."

"Oh, you have a sense of humour," Martin said. "You need it with the old gits here."

"Speak for yourself," Art said. "So have you?" He looked at Andy.

"No," Andy said. "Not seen a body, no."

"Once I have sorted my stuff out," Martin said. "I have a viewing booked for nine, I'll bring you in before the relatives, how does that sound?"

"It's an old boy," Art said. "Died peacefully in his sleep."

"What's a viewing?" Andy asked curiously.

"The body is laid out for the relatives to see," Art said. "They are dressed in the clothing selected by the family."

"Up to you," Martin said. "You are going to see a body or two, but if you prefer I can make sure you don't."

"No," Andy said. "I want the full experience," He nodded. "Treat me like an employee."

"Just don't beat this one," Art said bluntly.

"Look," Martin chuckled. "I hit you once!"

"Twice," Art said.

"Funny," Martin rolled his eyes. "Could you get the body ready for me?"

"Sure," Art said. "Let me put the keys away and I'll get started."

"If you wait here," Martin said to Andy. "I will be down shortly."

Andy nodded.

The small waiting room has two large three-seater couches on both sides of the room, black material with red cushions at each corner. In the middle is a large coffee table with a bible placed in the centre. The walls and ceiling are brilliant white, and the thick light grey carpet is immaculate.

Andy stood in front of a door next to Martin, his hands behind his back.

"The room is quite cool," Martin said. "For obvious reasons."

"Which is?" Andy asked curiously.

"We don't want to warm up a body," Martin shook his head in disgust. "Not a good thing."

"That is true," Andy said.

"So some rules before we go in," Martin said. "Don't touch the body or anything around the body."

"Do relatives?" Andy said.

"Yes," Martin said. "We advise against it, especially with makeup being used in most cases."

"Okay," Andy said.

"Any questions?" Martin asked. "You don't have to stay long, just walk in and have a look."

"No," Andy said. "All good."

Martin opened the door and stepped in, moving to the side as Andy followed.

The body of a man in his sixties is laid out on the wooden trolley, he is wearing a black suit, a light shirt, and a black tie. His head rests on a small white pillow, the trolley has a thin mattress, covered with a cream-patterned sheet. Behind the trolley is a large window, covered with a white slatted blind. The walls and ceiling are magnolia, the lighting warm and dimmed. A cabinet on one side of the room with candles, a silver cross and a bible at the end. Two wooden chairs with leather cushioned seats are on the other side of the room.

"Oh that is a nice chill," Andy said softly.

"I have to say it is quite nice at this time of the year," Martin said. "Especially when it is warm."

Andy nodded.

"This is Harold," Martin said. "His funeral is tomorrow and you will be helping out with that one."

"How did he die?" Andy asked. "Am I allowed to ask that?"

"Old age," Martin said. "Died in his sleep."

"Good way to go," Andy said, looking at the body and then grinning. "Nice try."

"What?" Martin said and turned.

"He isn't dead," Andy scoffed.

"He is," Martin said trying not to laugh.

"I can see his chest moving," Andy shook his head. "And the hairs on his nose are moving."

The man sat up from the trolley, laughing.

"Told you!" The man said laughing.

"Andy," Martin said. "Meet Gerald."

Gerald swung his legs around on the trolley, groaning as he stood up, his hand going to his hip.

"I knew that was going to happen," Gerald said. "My nephew is deaf, his attention to detail is amazing."

"I thought I saw your eyes move," Andy said. "But wasn't sure."

"You cannot even play a proper dead person," Martin scoffed. "Useless."

"I must admit I was trying not to let out a fart," Gerald said. Andy sniggered.

"You look dead most days anyhow," Martin said.

"Well we never know if you are alive most of the time," Gerald smirked, walking over to Andy, and holding out his hand. "Nice to meet you, Andy," He said.

Andy shook his hand.

"I will show you a real body shortly," Gerald said. "If you are okay with that?" He looked at Martin who nodded.

"Gerald will look after you this morning," Martin said. "He will also take you out to a coroner collection later this afternoon, but until then it will be the boring stuff."

"Doubt anything will be boring," Andy smiled.

"Give it time kid," Gerald said. "Give it time."

"Go grab a coffee and then get started," Martin said. "I will be heading out with Art and Paul."

"Do you not need me to coffin bear?" Gerald asked.

"No," Martin said. "The family have selected four bearers."

"When was that agreed?" Gerald asked. "As far as Marcia is concerned, we are all needed."

"Changed about ten minutes ago," Martin said. "Relatives called and added the change."

"Didn't need me in after all," Gerald said.

"At last you can look after Andy," Martin said. "You are a perfect person to show him the ropes."

"I suppose," Gerald said. "Got to let the adults do the work haven't we."

"Funny," Martin said. "Don't give up the day job!"

"Let's get a coffee," Gerald said. "You had breakfast?"
Andy nodded.

Andy sat down at the small wooden breakfast table, looking around the small room. The table is against the wall and behind it a small kitchen with a sink, cupboards, microwave, toaster, and refrigerator. On the other side of the room a small television on an old wooden table. On the old, yellow-painted walls are various photographs, pictures, and flyers.

"So Andy," Gerald said placing a mug of white coffee and a plate with a bacon sandwich in front of Andy. "Hold old are you?"

"Seventeen," Andy said.

"Is this something you are interested in?" He said returning to the kitchen, picking up a mug and plate before returning to the table and sitting down.

"How do you mean?" Andy said.

"Do you want to do this when you leave school?" Gerald asked.

"I have other plans," Andy said. "This is an interest."

"What are your plans?" Gerald asked.

"Performing arts," Andy said. "I want to get into acting."

"Oh that sounds interesting," Gerald nodded, biting into the bacon sandwich. "Eat up," He indicated towards the sandwich in front of Andy.

"Planning to go to a college closer to home," Andy said. "I live in Kent."

"Why are you doing work experience in Brighton?" Gerald asked. "Seems a long trek."

"I go to boarding school here," Andy said.

"Boarding school for the deaf?" Gerald said. "Near the blind place?"

"Yes," Andy nodded.

"Your speech is good," Gerald wiped his mouth. "Were you born deaf?"

"No," Andy said. "Went deaf at seven."

"How come?" Gerald asked. "If you don't mind me asking."

"No one knows," Andy said. "It just happened, one ear overnight and the other over a month."

"Did your parents look into why it happened?" Gerald said. "See any specialists?"

"No," Andy said. "They were a little put out about having a disabled son."

"You are kidding?" Gerald exclaimed.

"Afraid not," Andy said. "It's a long story, don't want to bore you with it."

"That sounds rough," Gerald said, moving his leg and groaning.

"You okay?" Andy asked.

"Bad leg," Gerald said. "Had a bad accident several years back."

"Sorry to hear that," Andy said. "What happened if you don't mind me asking?"

"It's an interesting story," Gerald said. "Not squeamish are you?"

"Nope," Andy smiled, biting into the bacon sandwich.

"I used to help out in Germany," Gerald said. "With a friend's undertaker business. It was a cold morning in February and we were on the way to a funeral, about an hour's drive. Body in the back and everything," He took a bite from his sandwich and a sip of coffee. "There is me, the hearse driver and another pallbearer," Gerald said. "Shit," He scoffed. "I cannot remember his name!"

The door opened and Leanne walked in, smiling at them both.

"Good morning Leanne," Gerald said. "You well?"

"Bit of a headache," Leanne said. "but not too bad."

"Messy weekend?" Gerald laughed.

"Very," She said. "Went to a Hen night on Saturday but didn't finish until Sunday morning."

"Owch," Gerald groaned. "You getting married?"

"No," Leanne placed the mugs in the sink. "A friend is," She groaned, her hand going to her stomach. "Will do those in a bit," She said, leaving the room in a hurry.

"Booze huh," Gerald said shaking his head. "Where was I?"

"Motorway in Germany," Andy said, finishing his sandwich.

"Oh yes," Gerald said. "On the way there, a truck managed to sideswipe us, and the hearse lost control, unfortunately flipping us."

"Shit!" Andy said.

"I was thrown from the hearse," Gerald explained. "Broke my leg and hip when I landed, a few ribs, also my back and my jaw."

"That must have hurt!" Andy shook his head.

"Not at first," Gerald said. "Shock. The driver was killed instantly, snapped neck" Gerald said and paused. "The other pallbearer was trapped in the wreckage."

"Sorry to hear that," Andy said.

"When I came to," Gerald said. "A police officer was attending to me," Gerald finished his sandwich. "And another was doing chest compressions," He let out a sigh." "On the body."

"No!" Andy exclaimed. "Could he not tell?!"
Gerald nodded.

"Mouth to mouth too," Gerald said. "No idea why the poor sod never caught on at that point."

"Lovely," Andy groaned, pulling a disgusted face.

"No idea what was going through the coppers head," Gerald said. "but with my broken jaw, it was extremely hard for me to explain what had happened," He smirked. "And what was happening."

"I guess he worked it out in the end?" Andy said.

"Yes," Gerald chuckled. "Spent a few minutes throwing up on the side of the road."

"That is bad," Andy said. "How was the guy trapped in the hearse?"

"He was okay," Gerald said with a nod. "Was the only sensible one wearing a seatbelt."

"Did the funeral go ahead?" Andy laughed. "Or was it cancelled due to the road trip?"

"It was delayed," Gerald said. "but it went ahead the same day, and the family had no idea what had happened that morning."

"Imagine being in a deadly car crash after you die," Andy said. "Did the family find out?"

"No," Gerald said. "The company sent another hearse along with a replacement coffin."

"Messy," Andy said.

"I know," Gerald scoffed. "I was in the hospital a while after that, had a few surgeries, my wife was happy about the jaw, while it lasted."

"That is a lot to deal with," Andy said. "Thanks for the sandwich."

"You are welcome," Gerald said and stood up, picking up the plates. "My wife prepares enough for everyone on a Monday," Gerald said walking over to the sink and running the hot tap. "She used to run a café and I think she misses it, to be honest."

"It was good," Andy said. "Why did she stop doing it?"

"She retired," Gerald said. "Sold the café and focused on adopting dogs."

"Oh wow," Any said.

"Now it's cats," Gerald moaned. "Cannot stand the sods."

"Bet you love them really," Andy said.

"Maybe one or two," Gerald said. "Have you been given a tour?" Gerald asked.

"Only the offices and the rooms from earlier," Andy said.

"I will show you the workshop," Gerald said. "And then the morgue," Gerald turned the tap off, putting the plates into the sink. "And the garage where we keep the vehicles."

"Sounds good," Andy said.

"We will head to the coroner's office around lunchtime," Gerald said. "Okay with you?"

Andy nodded.

"Good," Gerald said. "Finish your coffee and I'll give you a tour."

The door opened and Leanne walked in.

"You okay?" Gerald asked.

"Yeah," Leanne nodded. "Won't be drinking for a while."

"Heard that before!" Gerald laughed.

"I am serious," Leanne nodded.

"Sure you are," Gerald nodded.

"Did Andy tell you what happened earlier?" Leanne said.

"No," Gerald said looking at Andy who was confused.

"What happened earlier?" Andy asked.

"He was on the intercom this morning," Leanne said. "Explaining he was deaf and I thought he said his name was deaf!"

"Oh bloody hell!" Gerald moaned.

Andy started to laugh.

"Thought Andy was supposed to be the deaf one!" Gerald said shaking his head.

"I am really sorry Andy!" Leanne said, her hand over her mouth.

"What?" Andy said. "Cannot lipread you with your mouth covered."

"Shit," Leanne scoffed. "I am not very good at this am I?"

"You will be fine," Andy said. "Takes time."

"Right," Gerald said. "I need to give this lad a tour and then show him the morgue."

"Seen a body yet?" Leanne asked nervously.

"No not yet," Andy said.

"Tell him about your first time," Gerald said and chuckled softly.

"No!" Leanne moaned. "Does everyone need to know?"

"Yes," Andy said grinning. "I need to learn as much as I can."

"Oh god!" She muttered. "You guys are mean!"

"Go on," Gerald crossed his arms, leaning against the wall. "Tell him."

Leanne let out a frustrated sigh.

"On my first day I was supposed to help out with a funeral," She explained. "Being new and everything, but I was under the weather," She looked at Gerald and pointed. "With flu!"

"We know!" He said holding up his hands in defence.

"Anyway," She said. "I thought I was okay and they took me to the morgue and showed me the body of a guy and I came over a little dizzy."

"Threw up, fell forward and cracked her head on the trolley," Gerald laughed. "I spent a few hours in the hospital with her."

"Shit!" Andy exclaimed. "Were you okay?"

"I was okay," Leanne said. "Minor cut but I was embarrassed more than anything."

"Gave you quite the scare," Gerald shook his head.

"I thought I was pregnant!" Leanne gasped. "That would have messed up everything."

"Don't you go doing that," Gerald said.

"What?" Andy said. "Getting pregnant?"

"No you wally," Gerald rolled his eyes. "Passing out. I am not taking you to the hospital as well!"

"No chance," Andy said. "I'll be fine."

The refrigeration unit with fifteen numbered compartments is against the wall and a large metal trolley is at the centre of the room. The walls are bare bricks, the floor concrete and worn with time. The ceiling is white with two sets of fluorescent lights, bright harsh light. There is an entrance to the room opposite the refrigeration units, and on the left side a large window, with metal grills on both sides. On the right are two large cabinets, locked, a door in the middle of them. Andy stood in front of the large refrigeration unit with his arms crossed.

"Right Andy," Gerald said. "Sure you are okay to do this?"

"Yes," Andy nodded with a smile.

"Pick a number from the middle section," Gerald said. "Apart from number six."

"Why not six?" Andy asked.

"It's a child," Gerald said. "I don't want to see her, breaks my heart."

"Oh sorry," Andy said apologetically.

"It's not your fault," Gerald smiled. "No need to say sorry, it's very sad."

"Seven will do," Andy said.

"Why did I know you were going to say that," Gerald laughed and got hold of the trolley, grunting as he positioned it in front of compartment number seven. "This is a trolley we use for moving the bodies from the refrigerator," Gerald explained. "We can lower it and raise it to the levels we need," He pointed to a display at the front of the handles. "It also has a scale, but that doesn't work," He scoffed. "Still waiting on that to be repaired."

"Why is there a scale on it?" Andy asked.

"In case we need to weigh a body," Gerald said. "Helps us plan for pallbearing too."

"What?" Andy said. "Pull what?"

"Pallbearing," Gerald said.

"What is that?" Andy asked curiously.

"The people that carry a coffin," Gerald said. "Usually four in total, but all depends, sometimes six."

"Ah," Andy nodded. "I get it."

"Okay number seven," Gerald said and walked up to the side of the refrigerator and pulled the magnetic clipboard off the side. "Let's have a look."

Andy looked around the room, looking up at the lighting.

"It's nice and cool in here," Andy said.

"It really is," Gerald said. "It wasn't a few years back when the electrics failed," Gerald groaned. "Slap bang in the middle of summer and the smell wasn't great."

"I bet," Andy pulled a disgusted face.

"They only found out when one of the guys came on-site to do some work," Gerald said. "Okay number seven is a male in his thirties," Gerald said. "Suicide."

"That is sad," Andy said.

"It is," Gerald nodded in agreement. "Pills and alcohol."

"Poor guy," Andy said softly.

"Yeah," Gerald said. "Found by his partner."

"Not good," Andy said shaking his head.

Gerald opened the door to the compartment, pulling the latch sharply, a metallic clunk echoing through the room. Reaching in he grabbed hold of the tray, pulling it onto the trolley, the rollers inside the refrigerator clattering loudly. The tray is covered in a thick white sheet, the feet and the top of the head exposed. The long black hair is combed back neatly.

"Don't attempt this on your own," Gerald said. "I have years of experience."

"Will do," Andy said.

"We had a new guy start with us last year," Gerald paused, sighing deeply. "He got a bit cocky and decided to get in early and prepare a viewing," He chuckled, shaking his head. "The body was a large woman and he hadn't lined up the trolley properly."

"Splat?" Andy said.

"Splat indeed," Gerald scoffed. "By the time we had come in he was a mess, the body was on the floor, in a bad state that we had to call our embalmer to put things right."

"Oh dear," Andy said.

"That was his first warning," Gerald said. "He was fired on his second."

"What happening on his second," Andy said in interest.

"Lied about having a driving license," Gerald said. "Reversed the hearse into the bollard out the front," Gerald said. "If you look at it later, you can still see the dent and missing paint."

"Bloody hell," Andy scoffed.

"You drive?" Gerald asked.

"Had a couple of lessons," Andy said. "But not going very well, the instructor isn't very understanding."

"About what?" Gerald asked curiously.

"Deafness," Andy said. "I explained I am deaf, and said could we use signals and so on, but every time I am driving he keeps talking to me, and then has a go when I don't respond."

"That sounds unfair," Gerald said.

"Going to learn back home," Andy said. "Learning in Brighton is nuts."

"All the one-way streets!" Gerald exclaimed. "Even I still have trouble!"

"Was the hearse fixable?" Andy asked curiously.

"Yes," Gerald said. "We had to hire one for a while so it was expensive."

"Don't worry," Andy said. "I won't be touching it."

The door opened and Martin walked in, looking at both Andy and Gerald.

"Stealing bodies again Gerald?" Martin asked.

Gerald laughed.

"Has he told you he steals bodies?" Martin said seriously.

Andy looked at Gerald curiously.

"Ignore him," Gerald said. "Everyone else does."

"Oh no," Andy said. "You have to tell me everything."

"Go on," Martin said. "I want to know too."

"Basically," Gerald said looking at Andy. "He sucks at communication."

"A couple of years back when I was an undertaker," Martin said. "I got a body out for a viewing, after it was done, I went back to find the body missing."

Gerald laughed softly, covering his mouth.

"I went mad, running all over trying to find the body, checking the cold storage," Martin said. "Lastly I had to tell Marcia."

"That is where it got funny," Gerald said.

"I went to her office and she went nuts," Martin said. "Threatening me with the police and said my life was over, I was shitting myself!"

"Marcia asked me to transport the body to another site," Gerald said. "But kept that from Martin to see his skills."

"The horrible cow was in on it," Martin scoffed. "They let it go on for a few hours until they told me, they even said the police would investigate me!"

Andy burst out laughing.

"We had to stop because he was nearly in tears!" Gerald said. "We even got the local police officer to pop in for the fun of it!"

"Shit," Andy said. "Looks like there are constant wind-ups here."

"Always," Martin said. "Makes the day go quicker."

"Remind me to tell you about when Martin dressed up as Superman at a kid's funeral we did," Gerald said. "A story for another time."

Andy looked at Gerald, his mouth opened in amazement.

"What?" Martin asked curiously.

"We had the same look on our faces," Gerald said.

"Sounds like a comedy," Andy said.

"Wasn't far off," Martin said. "How everyone could keep a straight face, I will never know."

"Long and funny story," Gerald said. "I'll tell you later."

"Thanks," Martin said bluntly.

"No problems," Gerald said grinning. "We have to put up with you so it's only fair!"

42

"He is thawing out," Martin said. "Chop chop," He pointed to the body.

Gerald gently folded back the white sheet to reveal the pale body of the man, his long hair combed back, recently washed. Gerald stopped just past the chest, revealing the thick raw scars from the recent autopsy and embalming.

"Any questions?" Gerald asked.

"Doesn't look real," Andy said. "Looks like a waxwork model."

"The incisions you see on his torso," Martin pointed.

"Autopsy," Andy butted in.

"I'll shut up," Martin smiled.

"Could probably arrange to watch one," Gerald said. "If you are interested."

"Really?" Andy said with a grin. "That would be cool."

"I will see what I can do," Martin said. "Will leave you both to it."

Gerald nodded as Martin left the room in a hurry.

"Seen enough?" Gerald asked.

"Yes," Andy said.

"Cover him up then," Gerald indicated to the body. "Just unfold the sheet and roll it up."

Andy stepped forward, leaning over as he rolled up the sheet, pausing when he got to the man's neck.

"Not tucked a dead body in before," Andy said with a grin.

"Why don't I believe you?" Gerald said softly.

Andy covered the head and stepped back as Gerald pushed the tray into the refrigerator.

"Just a heads up that bodies don't always look like this," Gerald said as he closed the latch, pulling the trolley away. "Some look pretty beaten up, decomposed."

"What is the worst you have seen?" Andy asked curiously.

"Probably a kid," Gerald said. "Poor little sod got run over by his grandfather. Wasn't a good view."

"Owch," Andy said. "Sounds horrible."

"It was," Gerald said. "Very emotional day for all of us," Gerald let out a long sigh. "I'll show you around and then you can help me with an uplift if you are okay with that?"

"What is an uplift?" Andy asked.

"Collection from the hospital," Gerald said. "An old boy."

"Sure," Andy nodded.

"You bring lunch?" Gerald asked.

"No," Andy said. "Was going to pop to the shop down the road."

"You vegetarian or anything?" Gerald asked.

"I had bacon sandwiches with you this morning," Andy said laughing.

"That you did," Gerald scoffed and shook his head. "I am getting old, leave me alone. Anyway," Gerald said. "We order sandwiches from the local bakery, what do you fancy?"

"I don't mind," Andy said.

"You might regret that," Gerald said.

"It's a learning curve," Andy said.

"Okay," Gerald nodded and slowly smiled. "Let's finish your tour."

Andy stood outside the door with Gerald, the small black van parked behind them. They are parked up in a loading bay, facing an old shutter, rusty and stained. Gerald wore a black suit jacket.

"Are you not hot?" Andy asked. "I am melting!"

"Ah you get used to it," Gerald said. "Full dress is expected, regardless of the weather."

"Full dress?" Andy said curiously.

"Yes," Gerald said. "Complete uniform."

"Oh right," Andy nodded. "I'll remember my jacket tomorrow."

"Was going to ask if you had one," Gerald said. "We have some spares upstairs."

"Okay," Andy said.

"This is the morgue," Gerald said. "Sure you want to come in?" Andy nodded.

"Not planning on stealing any bodies are you?" Gerald asked.

"No," Andy said. "That is reserved for Fridays so I have the whole weekend."

"Psycho!" Gerald exclaimed and pressed the intercom. It rang out for several seconds before buzzing.

"Yes?" A woman's voice came over loudly.

"Your favourite person here," Gerald said.

"Pizza delivery guy?" The woman replied.

"Funny," Gerald scoffed. "Okay," He said. "Your second favourite person."

"Chinese delivery guy?" The woman said.

"It's Gerald, open the door, I have a visitor," Gerald said bluntly.

"Dead or alive?" She asked.

Gerald looked at Andy who looked confused and shrugged his shoulders.

"Alive," Gerald said. "Although he is pretty dark, so who knows."

"He sounds like he is going to be my third favourite person!" The woman exclaimed. "You brought me any food?"

"Yes, just open the bloody door!" Gerald moaned.

"You should have started with that," The woman said. "Always start with food."

The door clicked and Gerald pushed it open.

"Go on," Gerald said to Andy who walked through.

On the left is a door leading to the refrigeration storage, and directly ahead a door leading to the offices and hospital access. On the right, a door leads to a small office with a reception window on the side, covered in various printouts. The old green tiled floor is marked and worn from years of use. The flaking cream-coloured walls were dented, scraped, and discoloured. The fluorescent lights, running down the hall, were dim and flickering.

"Place needs an uplift," Gerald said. "Probably older than you are!"

"Yeah," Andy nodded. "What is that smell?"

"Disinfectant," Gerald said.

"I like it," Andy said.

"You would, bloody weirdo!" Gerald scoffed and laughed.
The door to the office opened and a heavily built woman stepped out, with short black hair and glasses wearing dark green scrubs and blood-splattered white clogs.

"Learning from the best is he?" The woman said. "Nice to meet you," She held out her hand. "I am Sonja, with a J."

"Hi," Andy shook her hand. "With a J?" He looked at her and then at Gerald in confusion.

"Yes, the J is actually pronounced with a Y," Gerald said with a smile. "Don't ask, she likes to be awkward."

"Okay," Andy nodded.

"New worker?" She asked Gerald.

"Andy is doing work experience with us for a week," Gerald said. "Just a week isn't it?" He asked Andy."

"Yes," Andy said.

"What made you want to work with the miserable gits at Grange Funerals?" Sonja said with a mischievous grin.

"Who are you calling miserable?" Gerald said handing a small brown paper bag to Sonja.

"Do you agree?" Sonja asked Andy.
Andy shook his head.

"Leave me out of this," Andy said. "I have to work with them for the week!"

"What are you bribing me with this time?" Sonja opened the bag and looked inside, breathing in deeply. "Bacon sarnies!"

"The wife thought you might like them," Gerald said. "She sends her love."

"Aww she is a star," Sonja chuckled. "Still don't get why she married you."

"Charm and good looks," Gerald said confidently.
Andy scoffed and laughed. Gerald looked at him, mouth open in mock shock.

"Who's side are you on?" Gerald exclaimed. "I am the one driving you back."

"I'll drop you back," Sonja said. "I like this one already," She gently punched Gerald in the arm.

"You are going to have to come round for dinner soon," Gerald said. "Bring your other half."

"She will like that," Sonja nodded. "So how can I help you?" Gerald pulled a folded sheet of paper from his pocket, handing it to Sonja.

"Collection," Gerald said.

"Let's go through," Sonja pointed to the double doors leading to the refrigerated storage. "Are you okay to join us, Andy?"

"Yes," Andy said.

"He is just as bad as you," Gerald said. "Not a squeamish bone in his body."

Andy grinned with excitement.

"As bad as me?" Sonja said. "What do you mean by that?"

"Mental," Gerald said confidently. "Absolutely flipping mental." Sonja punched him playfully in the arm as she approached the doors, opening them and holding them open for Andy and Gerald.

The strong smell of disinfectant hit Andy as he walked into the room. Twice the size of the refrigeration room at the undertakers, it is older and very outdated. The floors are tiled, previously white, but now a hint of yellow from years of use. The walls to the front and sides are plain bricked, the wall against the entrance plaster boarded with three large whiteboards mounted, recently installed. Against the wall on the opposite side are forty refrigerated units, stainless steel with tags hanging from the handles. In the centre of the room are two height-adjustable trolleys, one with a body on it, covered with a white sheet. On the left are double doors leading to the loading bay and on the right of the room, double doors leading to the hospital corridor. In the corner of the room is an old wooden desk with a computer on it, next to it is a large metal cabinet with a sign on the front stating 'Scrubs and Odds'. Next to that is a washbasin, above it are various racks with a selection of gloves.

"Is this the collection?" Gerald pointed to the body.

"No," Sonja said. "He came in about ten minutes ago, one of ours."

"Oh no," Gerald said. "Sorry to hear that. "Who is he?"

"Antony," Sonja said. "Used to work in special baby care."

"Don't think I know him," Gerald said.

"Let me jog your memory," Sonja said, walking over to the trolley and lifting the sheet to reveal a full tattooed arm sleeve."

"Oh I know who you mean," Gerald said. "That is a shame, he was a great guy!"

Gerald turned to Andy.

"He worked here for quite some time, always used to come down with parents of deceased babies," Gerald said. "Gentle guy."

"The tattoos used to make people uncomfortable," Sonja said. "But once people got to know the real him, they didn't take notice," Sonja said and pulled the sheet down to the torso, revealing a heavily tattooed chest, abdomen, and both arms.

"Bloody hell," Gerald said. "He liked his tattoos!"

"I like the sleeves," Andy said.

"Got any?" Sonja asked.

"No," Andy said. "Not yet."

"What happened?" Gerald asked. "What was he, early forties?"

"Cardiac arrest," Sonja said. "Came into work as normal yesterday, came over ill and collapsed. They managed to revive and stabilize him and took him to Cardiac Care, but he was arrested early this morning and they couldn't do anything for him."

"Shit Sonja," Gerald said. "I am sorry to hear that."

"Healthy guy," She said. "Didn't smoke or drink, ran every day and also a vegetarian."

"Must have had some underlying issues?" Gerald said. "Are they doing anything for him?"

"We are doing a collection," Sonja said. "I think his partner just had another baby."

"That is sad," Andy said.

"Very," Gerald said.

Sonja covered up the body, resting her hand on his chest.

"Anyhow," She took a deep breath. "Let's get you sorted, I am sure you are busy doing nothing all day!"

Andy laughed.

"Cheeky git!" Gerald said looking at him. "Will bloody leave you here!"

"That is okay," Andy said. "Buses run from outside the hospital," He grinned.

"Got a spare refrigerator I can lock him in?" Gerald asked Sonja.

"Leave him alone you antique!" Sonja scolded him.

Sonja unlocked the empty trolley and pushed it up to one of the refrigerated compartments, the metallic clunk echoing around the room when the trolley hit the frame.

"This guy was discharged a couple of weeks ago after elective surgery," Sonja said. "Fell down the stairs and died, was a week until he was found."

"Jesus!" Gerald said softly.

"Not a pretty sight," Sonja sighed as she opened the door. "Or smell," She looked at Andy. "Do you want a mask?"

"For what?" Andy asked curiously.

"The smell?" Sonja said. "It's not nice."

"Worse than rotten liquified chicken?" Andy asked.

"Definitely not!" Sonja groaned. "Rotten chicken is the worst!"

"Probably all the chemicals they use to make them fatter," Gerald said. "If it is too much," He said to Andy. "You can wait outside?"

"I will be fine," Andy said.

"The family may want a viewing," Sonja said. "He recently became a grandfather for the first time."

"Poor sod," Gerald said. "What killed him?"

Sonja pulled out the tray, pulling the body onto the trolley and then wheeling the trolley back to the centre. She closed the compartment door and then pulled the sheet back to reveal the body of a man in his mid-sixties, short, bald, and slightly overweight. His glazed eyes are open and his jaw is distorted.

"Broke his neck," Gerald said and sighed.

"And his jaw," Sonja said. "So that is why I wouldn't recommend a viewing."

"The family have requested one," Gerald said and moved closer. "Amanda will work her magic."

"How is she doing?" Sonja asked. "Not seen her in ages."

"She is good," Gerald said. "Self-employed now," Gerald faced Andy. "Amanda is our embalmer and makeup specialist, she does some amazing work!"

"She joined the undertakers as an admin officer and hated it, so they put her with the miserable sods as an undertaker," Sonja smiled. "Changed her life."

"We sponsored her and got her trained up in embalming," Gerald said. "She is doing well."

"She is absolutely raking it in too," Sonja said. "Give her my love."

"Will do," Gerald said looking at his watch. "Better get moving, you talk too much!" He rolled his eyes at Sonja.

"Those will fall out if you keep rolling them," Sonja said. "I am surprised your head hasn't taken off!"

Andy burst out laughing, his hand going to his mouth as he looked at Gerald.

"What are you laughing at?" Gerald asked him. "It's almost like you want to walk back."

"That was funny," Andy said grinning.

"Do I roll my eyes much?" Gerald asked him.

"Well I get dizzy just lipreading you," Andy replied.

Sonja laughed and then started to cough.

"Keep going," Gerald encouraged Andy. "Maybe you will kill her!"

"No Chance," Sonja said. "I will be here long after you are dead."

"That's a witch for you," Gerald said to Andy. "Be careful this one doesn't put a curse on you!"

"How can I be a witch when I am cursed?" Sonja questioned Gerald.

"Cursed?" Gerald exclaimed. "How are you cursed?"

"With you!" Sonja stuck her tongue out.

"So I guess I should tell my other half to stop sending the Bacon Sarnies?" Gerald said. "Considering I am a curse?"

"Try it," Sonja pointed at him.

"That hit a nerve!" Andy said laughing.

"Threaten me with anything but food," Sonja said. "He hasn't learned."

"Okay back to work," Gerald said. "Shutter working yet?"

"Still down," Sonja said. "Still signed off by the health and safety official."

"Bloody useless," Gerald scoffed. "How hard is it to get a shutter fixed?"

"What's up with it?" Andy asked.

"The control box failed," Sonja said. "So for a while, we have used the manual chain, but a few weeks ago one of the porters lost a couple of fingers and broke his wrist due to someone messing around."

"Turns out one of the younger porters thought it would be funny to pull the chain down as hard as he could," Gerald said. "So when the unlucky sod opened it, it yanked his hand through the guard."

"We all heard the crash followed by a scream," Sonja said. "Hell of a mess."

"Is he getting a payout?" Gerald asked.

"Oh yes," Sonja said. "That is why it's out of commission."

"I'll get the trolley," Gerald said.

"Need any help?" Andy asked.

"No I am good," Gerald said. "It's designed for one person to operate."

"Tight bastards," Sonja laughed. "Cutting down on the manpower!"

Gerald shook his head and left the room, letting the door close heavily behind him.

"How are you finding it?" Sonja asked.

"Not too bad," Andy said. "Only the first day."

"The guys are pretty cool," Sonja said with a chuckle. "I am not sure they take anything seriously."

"It's been a fun-filled day so far," Andy said.

"You working with the undertaking team or upstairs too?" Sonja said.

"Just the undertaking team as far as I know," Andy replied. "Not too keen on office work."

"You met Marcia?" Sonja asked.

"Yes," Andy replied. "Don't find her as scary as everyone is making her out to be."

"Oh, she is a teddy bear!" Sonja exclaimed. "Until someone swears!"

Andy nodded in understanding.

"She has made a fortune in fines with the guys and their swearing!" She said sniggering. "They constantly bait each other now when she hovers!"

"I'll watch out for that," Andy said.

"You should ask Martin how his nose is," Sonja said with a smile.

"His nose?" Andy said, confused.

"A month after he started," Sonja explained. "Martin tried his luck with Marcia, dropping the odd swear word and blaming it on Tourette's."

"What is that?" Andy asked.

"Not heard of Tourette's?" Sonja said.

"No," Andy said shaking his head. "What is it?"

Sonja laughed and shook her head.

"It's a neurological condition that causes unwanted, involuntary muscle movements and sounds known as tics," She explained. "We used to have a porter that suffered from it."

"Oh right," Andy said nodding in understanding.

"He was laid off," Sonja said. "Management couldn't handle him telling staff and patients to fuck off."

Andy spluttered and laughed.

"No!" Andy exclaimed.

"Yeah," Sonja shook her head. "Poor sod couldn't help it and they pushed him out."

"Not fair," Andy said. "Did he fight?"

"Yes," Sonja said.

The door bashed open and Gerald pushed in a lightweight trolley, looking frustrated and red in the face.

"You need to get those automated doors fixed," He said. "Unless you actually want me to drop dead at the door?"

"As fun as that sounds," Sonja said holding the door open for him. "I am too busy to deal with another old man."

"What were you two banging on about?" Gerald asked curiously.

"Martins Tourette's," Sonja said. "When Marcia found out."

"I forgot about that!" Gerald laughed. "Got him a broken nose for his troubles."

Andy looked at both Gerald and Sonja in confusion.

"Marcia threw a bottle at him playfully after she realised he was messing around," Gerald scoffed. "Unfortunately, it caught him on the bridge of his nose with a crack."

"Directed his first funeral with two black eyes," Sonja sniggered. "I still have a photograph somewhere!"

There is a loud crash and the doors are pushed open by a porter pushing a trolley with a blue cover over the top of it. The tall, overweight porter is wearing navy blue trousers, a white shirt, and black boots. He has a face mask on, his long messy hair, hanging over his face. He grips the trolley with latex gloves.

"What have I said about bashing the doors open with the trolley!" Sonja complained. "Have some respect!" She groaned. "That's a bit raw!"

The smell of excrement hit all three of them as the airflow hit them from the corridor. Andy groaned, his hand going to his nose.

"Not my fault she shit herself," The porter moaned.

"They should have cleaned her up before she came down!" Sonja snapped. "You know that."

"Only doing what I am asked," The porter said brushing his hair back, not noticing the excrement on his hands.

"Oh, Jesus Christ!" Gerald scoffed. "You have got shit on your hair now."

"It's all over you!" Sonja pointed to his shirt. "You came all the way down from upstairs like that?"

The porter looked at his hand and groaned in annoyance.

"She had a stroke," He said. "Staff said it was like a chocolate waterfall!" He laughed.

"Enough of that!" Sonja said. "Go away."

"Need any help?" The porter asked.

"No!" Sonja snapped. "Just leave and make sure you clean up!" The porter scoffed, rolled his eyes, and stormed off, slamming the doors against the wall.

"What is his problem?" Andy asked.

"Does his own thing," Sonja said. "Let me move the poor girl." Gerald went to help Sonja but she held up her hand and shook her head.

"Better not," She said. "Just in case."

Andy cringed at the excrement trickling down the trolley and splattering onto the floor.

"That bothers you?" Gerald said noticing Andy pulling a face in disgust.

"Nothing worse than raw poo on a hot day," Andy shook his head.

"How about warm liquidised chicken?" Sonja asked.

"Oh no," Andy shivered. "That wins."

"I'll go and let Chris know," Gerald said. "Get him to get the cleaners down."

"We have a new guy," Sonja said. "He will do it, ask for Kim."

"Kim?" Gerald said curiously.

"Yeah," Sonja nodded.

"A guy," Gerald paused. "Called Kim?"

"Yes," Sonja scoffed. "Stop being a miserable bigot."

"My sister-in-law is called Kim," Gerald said. "Just seems odd."

"Employed him last week," Sonja said. "I asked for a general assistant to help out with the odds and ends in the morgue."

"How about getting him to fix the loading bay?" Gerald said with a smile.

"How about you shut up," Sonja warned him. "You want a coffee before you go?"

"No," Gerald said. "Want me to drop you back at the school?" He asked Andy.

"Isn't it out of your way?" Andy asked.

"It's only a few minutes," Gerald said. "Not a problem."

"You can drop me by the seafront," Andy said.

"No problems," Gerald said. "Let's get this lad in the van before he gets fed up with Sonja whining, gets up and walks out."

"You are an arse," Sonja said. "One day you will be on this trolley and I will be talking to you all day."

"That is the problem," Gerald nudged Andy. "The dead cannot talk back."

"Yet," Andy said.

"You watch too many films," Gerald said. "He is a horror nut like you, Sonja."

"My kind of people!" Sonja said. "Come on, get lost, the smell of raw crap is putting me off my dinner."

The van pulled up at the bus stop, the coast behind them. Dark clouds filled the skies and the sea was rough, the waves crashing against the rocks. Gerald groaned as he set the handbrake, taking the van out of gear, and shaking the gear stick a couple of times.

"So," He said looking in the side mirrors. "How was your first day?"

"Sorry?" Andy said looking at Gerald in confusion.

"I asked what you thought of your first day with us," Gerald said. "Are you coming back for more or have you had enough?"

"I am coming back for the bacon sandwiches!" Andy chuckled.

"Thought you might!" Gerald smiled. "Seriously, how are you finding it?"

"Loving it," Andy said. "Looking forward to doing more."

"Glad to hear it," Gerald said. "You are with Arthur tomorrow as I have a hospital appointment."

"Okay," Andy nodded.

"Do you want picking up in the morning?" Gerald asked. "Arthur lives in Rottingdean, so he passes this way."

"That would be good if it isn't a problem," Andy said. "I don't mind either way."

"How did you get in this morning?" Gerald asked. "Is there a school bus or something?"

"No," Andy said. "I got the bus from here into town and walked to the undertakers," Andy said stifling a yawn. "Could easily walk it from here."

"I will let Arthur know and he will pick you up," Gerald said. "He offered so don't stress about it."

"Thanks," Andy said. "You have all made me feel very welcome today."

"Ah," Gerald scoffed. "You wait until we feed you to the undead."

"That is no way to talk about Marcia!" Andy burst out laughing. "She isn't that bad."

"Give it time," Gerald said. "You have only seen the nice side of her. Well good to see you, and I will be in on Wednesday."

"Thanks again," Andy said and attempted to open the door, only for it to not open.

"It sticks," Gerald said. "Give it a shove."

Andy pulled the door latch, putting some pressure on the door.

"No," Andy said. "Won't let me out."

"Let me open it for you," Gerald said and got out of the van, walking round to the passenger side. Andy, not hearing what Gerald had said, leaned against the door and bumped it with his shoulder. As Gerald opened the door, Andy fell out and landed face down on the path. Gerald attempted to catch him, only to stumble backwards, nearly falling over.

"You okay lad?" Gerald said.

Andy groaned and got onto his knees, his hand going to his nose.

"You hurt?" Gerald said bending down, his hand on Andy's shoulder.

"What?" Andy said looking up at Gerald, blood trickling from his nose.

"Oh shit you are bleeding," Gerald said in worry. "Let me take you to the hospital."

"No," Andy said, wiping the blood from his lip and then licking it away. "I get nosebleeds all the time."

"You sure?" Gerald said. "You a vampire or something," he cringed at Andy licking the blood away from the back of his hand.

"Cannot tell you that," Andy laughed getting to his feet. "You okay?"

"I am fine," Gerald said. "You are the one that kissed the path." Andy laughed.

"I bounce," Andy said. "I am accident-prone anyhow!"

"Want me to drop you at the school?" Gerald asked.

"No," Andy said. "Going to spend some time on the seafront before I go back," Andy said. "Not a fan of the place to be honest."

"Why so?" Gerald asked.

"Bullies," Andy said. "One of the guys in my year has an obsession with making my life a misery."

"Reported him?" Gerald asked.

"No point," Andy said. "Family in high places, so the school won't do anything."

"That isn't on at all," Gerald huffed. "Sure you are okay?"

"I am fine," Andy said. "Thanks for the lift and I will see you on Wednesday."

"Okay if you are sure," Gerald said, patting Andy on the back. "I am on coffin workshop duties on Wednesday, so you can help me with that. I also want to move a few things around, make some room if you are good to help?"

"Would be happy to," Andy said smiling, and nodding as he started to walk away. "Bye."

"Take care," Gerald said and waved, getting into the van, and slowly pulling away.

Andy made his way towards the walkway under the main road, heading down the steps to the coast.

# TUESDAY

Andy sat back on the worn bench at a bus stop, the sun beating down made bearable by the sea breeze. He crossed his arms, yawning loudly. The bus stop is situated on the edge of a roundabout, a main road running in front of the seafront. Behind the bus stop is a large modern building with maintained gardens surrounding it. Further down the fields, an area set up for archery, four large targets set up.

"Good morning," A man said loudly.

"Jesus!" Andy yelped. "Where did you come from!" He scoffed, his hand going to his chest.

Andy looked at the tall slim man standing next to the bench wearing sunglasses, light grey trousers, a dark grey shirt, and black polished shoes.

"Sorry did I scare you?" The man laughed.

"Didn't see you there," Andy said. "Sorry."

"Did you not hear me coming?" The man asked.

"I am deaf," Andy said. "The noise of the traffic takes over."

"Ah sorry," The man said. "But that makes things funnier."

"How do you mean?" Andy asked curiously.

"Have a guess," The man said looking towards Andy with a grin on his face.

Andy shook his head.

"No idea," Andy said.

The man held up a folded white and red cane.

"I am blind," The man said.

"Oh! Andy said noticing. "I had no idea."

"It's a moment out of the film!" The man laughed.

"What film?" Andy said curiously.

"See no evil, hear no evil?" The man said, feeling the edge of the bench. "Is the seat clean?"

"Yes," Andy said checking. "What's the film about?"

"You really haven't seen it?" The man asked. "Then again, neither have I."

"But you have heard it I guess?" Andy shook his head.

"It's about a deaf guy and a blind guy, both witness a murder," The man said sitting down. "One hears it and the other sees it," He laughed. "It's funny."

"I'll keep an eye out for it," Andy said.

"Good," The man said. "You from the deaf boarding school?"

"Yes," Andy nodded. "What about you?"

"No," The man shook his head. "I am not from the deaf boarding school," He grinned.

"Are you from the blind school?" Andy said looking at the building behind him.

"I am a music teacher there," The man said.

"Oh cool," Andy said in interest. "What instruments?"

"Piano, guitar and violin," The man said. "Do you play anything?"

"I play the trumpet," Andy said. "Few other instruments but have no interest, cannot make out the sounds."

"I guess it's hard," The man said. "I am Jon by the way."

"Nice to meet you, Jon," Andy held out his hand. "I am Andy."

"Are you holding out your hand Andy?" Jon chuckled. "It's not a problem, just place it on mine so I know where it is."

Andy touched Jon's hand and he grabbed hold of it, shaking it firmly.

"What are you doing?" Jon asked. "bunking off?"

"No," Andy laughed. "I am on work experience."

"Oh that is interesting," Jon nodded. "What are you doing?"

"Have a guess," Andy said. "It's something different from the usual boring stuff."

"I am never going to get this," Jon scoffed. "Give me a clue."

"I get to meet loads of people," Andy said. "Not many of them talk or do much."

"That is no help," Jon said. "Give me another clue."

Andy sighed, thinking.

"Expensive cars," Andy said.

"We talking limousines?" Jon asked curiously.

"Yes," Andy said.

"Bodyguard?" Jon said curiously, laughing softly.

"No," Andy said. "But if involves bodies."

"Undertaker?" Jon said with confidence.

"Nice guess," Andy exclaimed.

"It's not a guess," Jon said. "I can smell the death on you."

"Really?" Andy said and sniffed his shirt, his face screwed up in confusion.

"No," Jon laughed. "Really was a guess."

"I am enjoying it," Andy said. "Probably worth looking into making a career of it."

"What are you planning on doing?" Jon turned and faced Andy. "When you finish school?"

"Performing Arts," Andy said. "I love acting but may also give stunt work a try."

"Sounds painful," Jon shook his head. "The stunt work I mean." Andy looked at the road when he noticed the undertaker's van pull into the road from the roundabout, coming to a stop on the opposite side of the road.

"That is me," Andy said and stood up. "Nice meeting you Jon."

"And you," Jon said, holding up his hand and waving. "Hope the future works out for you mate."

"Thanks," Andy said, looking both ways before running across the road, nodding at Arthur and Martin sitting in the front.

"Morning!" Arthur waved. "Hope you are ready for a fun-filled day?!"

Jon laughed, shaking his head.

"So," Andy said as he opened the door. "What do you two call fun?" Andy looked at his watch. "You are up early!"

Arthur burst out laughing, going quiet when Martin looked at him, unimpressed.

"Kid has a point," Arthur said. "I don't think I have seen you before eight."

"Ha bloody ha!" Martin scoffed. "Didn't I offer to get us all breakfast?"

"You did," Arthur nodded. "I give you that one."

Andy squeezed in next to Martin, trying to put the seatbelt on.

"Don't bother," Martin said. "It's broken."

"Well if I die," Andy said. "I don't have far to go."

Arthur slowly pulled out and did a quick U-turn causing Andy to groan when Martin leaned into him, pressing him up against the door.

"Giving you a choice Andy," Martin said. "You can either join us today on a collection, or we can drop you at the office."

"I'll join you," Andy said. "What is happening?"

"Body collection," Arthur said. "Elderly woman, paramedic confirmed her death and had to leave after her dog went for him."

"Shit!" Andy exclaimed.

"He was bitten pretty badly from what we heard," Martin said. "You up to date on your tetanus in case we send you after the dog?" He chuckled.

"Yes," Andy shrugged his shoulders. "Will bribe it with your breakfast."

"Seriously," Arthur said. "They need to get the dog under control before we go in."

"You may have to wait in the van," Martin said. "Depends on what the police say."

"It's likely to be gruesome," Arthur said. "Been dead a week or so."

"I am happy to join you," Andy said. "If I can."

"Will see how things go," Martin said.

"Did you tell Andy about the vacancy?" Arthur said.

"No," Martin said. "Not got round to confirming it."

"What is that?" Andy asked curiously.

"We have a job opening up," Martin said.

"I heard about the guy that got fired," Andy said. "Dropped a body and crashed the hearse."

Arthur started to laugh softly, shaking his head.

"He was an idiot," Martin said. "Kept us busy the day he dropped the body."

"It practically burst," Arthur said. "Literally like someone dropped a water balloon full of blood and bile."

Martin gagged.

"What's up with him?" Andy said.

"Bile," Arthur said.

Martin dry heaved, his hand going to his mouth.

"Don't you throw up in here," Arthur warned him. "Martin here can handle anything but digestive-related fluids."

"Please," Martin shook his head. "I tell you, I have seen so much, but no!" He gagged.

"Wasn't an issue before," Arthur said smiling. "All it took is a trip," Arthur paused. "Want me to tell the story?"

"No," Martin said shaking his and grinning in sarcasm. "I will."

"Is it gory?" Andy said in excitement.

69

"We had a collection from a house, old overweight guy died in the summer house," Martin took a deep breath, prompting Arthur to wind down the window.

"I was on that collection with him," Arthur said. "The body had been in the summer house a week or two, slap bang in the summer."

"Arthur went in while I spoke to the coroner and the police," Martin said reaching for a bottle of water, offering it to Andy who shook his head. "Anyhow," Martin sipped from the bottle. "They put it down to cardiac arrest due to his weight and the ton of pills he had in the house, once we signed off the paperwork, I grabbed the trolley," Martin groaned and shook his head. "You finish the story."

"Okay," Arthur chuckled. "Martin was rushing around due to the smell and trust me it was bad!"

"What was the smell?" Andy asked. "I guess it was bad, but what is the smell?"

"You will find out later," Arthur said. "Anyway, as Martin rushed in, a rake caught on his trousers and he tripped!" Arthur burst into hysterics.

"Come on!" Martin exclaimed. "It isn't funny!"

"He bounced off the wooden bar and went falling, hands first into the bloated and rotten abdomen of the body."

Martin groaned and gagged.

"By the time I could help him, he was in a state of shock with all kinds of juices running down his face," Arthur said. "Best I could do was hose his hands and face out the back."

"Police enjoyed the show didn't they?" Martin said breathing deeply.

"They did," Arthur said. "Poor Martin also broke a finger."

"Oh nasty," Andy said.

"Had to get a tetanus as well," Martin said. "Managed to cut my hand a little."

"What a mess," Arthur said. "The police were helpful in the end, especially that young lad."

"We doubt he had much choice," Martin said. "I was too busy throwing up."

"Got some in your mouth didn't you?" Arthur chuckled.

"Oh stop it!" Martin gagged.

"What is the worst you have smelt?" Arthur asked Andy.

"Chicken," Andy said. "Someone left a pack in the cupboard at work, no idea why, it fell on the worktop when I pulled out a plate and pretty much exploded," Andy groaned. "Splattered my top and my face, spent half an hour throwing up my guts!"

"Chicken is the worst!" Martin said. "Worse than some bodies I have smelt."

"Going to agree with you on that one," Arthur said.

" Can you stop at the garage on the way will you, I need to get something cold," Martin looked at his watch.

"Sure," Arthur said. "Then we need to get business sorted."

"If I am allowed," Andy said. "I am happy to go in for you."

"Brave sod," Arthur said. "Has no idea what we are walking into."

"No," Martin said. "I need to, it's my job."

"Garage," Arthur said. "Then the gristly crime scene."

"You make it sound interesting," Andy said. "Cannot wait!" he smiled.

The van pulled up at the cordoned-off road at the end of the street, terraced houses down both sides with cars parked on both sides of the road. One end of the street is blocked by a police van, and the opposite end is blocked by an ambulance, the lights flashing. One officer stood in front of the ambulance behind blue 'Police' tape that had been wrapped around the walls on both ends of the street. Several people had gathered, looking down at the house where another officer stood outside the gate.

"Not too busy," Martin said.

Martin now sat next to the passenger door, Andy in the middle. The police officer noticed the van, speaking into his radio before making his way towards it. He is wearing black trousers and a white shirt, a high visibility vest over the top. Tall and muscular, he slowly walks over.

"He comes the Hulk," Arthur said under his breath.

"What?" Any asked curiously.

"Will tell you later," Arthur smiled.

"Good morning," Martin said. "We are expected."

"I am aware," The officer said. "We are waiting on an armed response."

"How come?" Martin asked. "Water?" He offered a bottle of water to the officer who nodded, taking it from him and opening it, he quickly drank half of the bottle, sighing in relief.

"I needed that," The officer sighed. "It's warm this morning," He leaned against the van, looking down the street. "The dog bit a paramedic and the vet," The officer said, shaking his head. "Poor thing is scared shitless and protecting deceased."

"You guys call the vet?" Martin asked.

"No," The officer said. "He lives down the end, decided to offer the help, said he could handle it."

"Clearly not," Arthur said. "Are you Samuel?" Arther looked down a little.

"Yeah," Samuel said. "How did you know?"

"You used to play rugby with my nephew," Arthur said. "We met the day the kid cut his leg open."

"Bloody hell," Samuel scoffed. "Good memory!"

"Probably the only thing that works," Martin said. Arthur shook his head in disgust.

"Myself and the misses did the first aid," Arthur said. "Did that kid ever play again?"

Samuel shook his head.

"Some kid dived, and slid across the grass," Arther said looking at Andy who looked confused. "Turns out there was some glass, sliced his thigh open."

Andy hissed, his face twisted.

"I never saw him again," Samuel said. "Then again, I left after two months."

"Any more information?" Martin asked. "On the body?" He pulled out a notepad from the glove compartment.

"Paramedic says it looks like she fell, hit her head on packs of tinned dog food," Samuel said. "Compound fracture in her head and possible broken neck, he was about to have a closer look when the dog went for him," Samuel said. "Like something out of a horror film apparently."

"That brings a film to mind," Andy said slightly smiling.

"I bet it does," Martin shook his head.

"From what I have also been told," Samuel took a deep breath. "The dog has eaten some of her backside and thigh."

"Oh no!" Arther said, looking at Andy. "This might not be suitable to talk about around Andy."

"It's okay," Andy said. "Really."

"This is Andy by the way," Arthur said pointing to Andy. "He is on work experience with us for a week."

"You morbid or something mate?" Samuel chuckled. "Man, didn't anything else interest you?"

"This did," Andy said. "Would have joined the police, but they don't take in disabled people."
Samuel nodded.

"How long has she been there?" Martin asked.

74

"She was last seen on Wednesday last week, walking the dog," Samuel said. "Neighbour across the street is in bits because she didn't click on that something was wrong."

"What about next door?" Arthur said. "Surely the dog would have annoyed them?"

"A couple on one side are deaf," Samuel said. "The other side is on vacation."

"Sods law," Martin said. "Someone lurking at the back of our van," Martin looked in the mirror.

A man came up behind Samuel, holding a tape recorder. He is short and slim, balding, and wearing glasses, his grey trousers are tight and his white shirt is wet with perspiration.

"Could I get some answers to some questions?" He asked Samuel.

"No," Samuel said. "Until we have secured things and informed the next of kin, no."

"Anything you can give me would be great?" He said. "I work with the local newspaper."

"No," Samuel said. "Could you go away, please! "

"Only doing my job," The man said. "Can't you give me anything?"

"A ride in a police car?" Samuel said.

Arthur exclaimed and suppressed a giggle.

"Come on mate," Samuel said. "I will update you as soon as I have something," He looked at Martin. "I'll let you know when it's safe to access the building."

Martin nodded and gave Samuel a thumbs up, he then turned to Andy.

"Were you thinking of the same dog film that I was?" Martin asked.

"A rabid Saint Bernards?" Andy smiled. "Oh yes!"

"Another horror nut," Arthur said. "That is all we need."

"Have you been for a ride in a police car?" Martin looked at Arthur. "It can be arranged."

"Not in a while no," Arthur laughed. "What about you Andy?"

"A couple of years ago," Andy said.

Martin looked at Andy curiously.

"Really?" Martin said. "What did you do?"

"Killed a couple of people," Andy said. "Nothing too extreme."

Arthur chuckled and then looked at Martin with worry.

"Are you telling me we have a murderer in the van?" Martin said. "Unlikely there being two in the same van."

"Told you to keep that a secret!" Arthur said. "Damn you Martin."

"So what was the real reason?" Martin asked.

"Guess," Andy said.

"Shoplifting?" Martin asked.

"No," Andy said. "Nothing that boring."

"Oh bloody hell," Martin said. "Got us a nutcase."

"Come on," Arthur said. "Put us out of our misery."

"Only kidding," Andy said. "It was all a show for my uncle who is mentally handicapped, basically," Andy said. "We pulled up next

76

to a police car on the way dropping him off, the police officer rolled down the window for a chat, and my uncle told the officer I had drugs up my butt."

Arthur started laughing.

"So they put their lights on, pulled me out of the car and cuffed me before driving off," Andy said with a grin.

"That is cool!" Martin said, chuckling softly.

"They dropped me off at my uncle's care home," Andy said. "Kept him happy and he talked about it for weeks."

"Sounds like a laugh," Arthur said.

"Yeah," Andy said. "Telling everyone he met I hid drugs up my arse."

"You don't do you?" Martin teased. "Don't want any problems with Samuel over there, he is huge!"

A white Land Rover drove past, mounting the pavement as Samuel ran over, removing the police tape and speaking with the two officers in the vehicle.

"Gun squad," Martin pointed.

"Looks like they are going to shoot the dog," Arthur said.

"No way!" Andy said, gasping softly. "Poor dog."

"It's suffering," Arthur said. "It's nicer this way."

"Have they tried though?" Andy said. "To try and help it?"

"You heard the police officer," Arthur said. "It has bitten people," He sighed. "Imagine how long the poor thing has been alone with her?"

"Especially seeing as it has been eating her," Martin shivered. "Gives me the creeps."

"Seen it before?" Andy asked.

"What animals that have eaten people?" Martin said, sighing heavily and putting his head back, thinking. "Yeah, a couple."

"We had that young guy a couple of years ago," Arthur said. "The one in the woods."

"Oh yeah," Martin said. "That was brutal."

"Not forgetting the one with the old boy and the cats," Arthur said. "That has to be the worst for me."

"That was a mess," Martin said. "A couple of cats had died, so the others ate them, and then made a start on the old boy."

"Lovely," Andy said, a grin on his face.

"Maggots are common," Arthur said. "Circle of life and all that." Andy watched as the Land Rover parked up opposite the house and the two uniformed officers, both armed made their way towards the officer outside the house. After speaking for a few minutes, they made their way into the house.

"Can you hear that?" Martin asked Andy.

"No," Andy said. "What is it?"

"Dog is barking," Arthur said. "And snarling."

"Blimey," Andy said. "Poor thing must be freaked out."

"I bet," Martin said. "Only protecting his owner," He turned and faced Andy. "You got any pets?"

"No," Andy said. "You?"

"A fiancé," Martin chuckled.

"I am telling her you said that," Arthur said. "She is the only person that scares you."

"My mother does a good job," Martin said. "Wouldn't even be engaged if it hadn't been for her interfering.

A shot rang out and Andy jumped, it echoed down the street, causing several people to look in the direction of the house.

"That was loud," Arthur said. "You heard that didn't you?" He asked Andy.

Andy nodded, looking at the house.

"You okay?" Arthur said. "Freaked out?"

"Got a soft spot for animals," Andy said. "Don't like the idea that it had to die."

"Neither do I," Martin said. "But it was out of control."

"Let's get some fresh air," Arthur said, nudging Andy. "Come on."

Andy stood behind Arthur, trying to look into the hall of the house, catching a glimpse of the dog's body at the end of the hall, covered in a large towel. Martin spoke with a police officer and also a paramedic, his hand bandaged.

"Sure you are okay to come in?" Arthur asked. "You don't have to and no one will blame you if you want to sit it out?"

"No," Andy said. "It's fine."

"Okay," Arthur said. "As long as you are sure, but don't touch anything."

"The police and coroner have done their bit," Martin said. "They have requested we take her to the local hospital, so they can do an autopsy and so on," Martin looked at the police officer. "I am just explaining the process to Andy," He said.

"Fine," The officer said. "All good."

"Let's get this over and done with," Arthur said. "I am hungry."

"Always a weird one," Martin rolled his eyes. "You will be glad you haven't eaten yet."

Andy nodded, moving out of the way as the paramedic gently pushed through, holding his hand.

"Ready?" Martin said. "You may want a mask, it's pretty strong." Andy removed a mask from his pocket, watching Arthur as he put his one on and then copied him, pinching it tightly around the nose.

"Andy," Martin said. "Just observe and don't touch anything please."

"I have explained everything to him," Arthur said. "He is just going to watch."

"If it becomes too much and you want to leave, then please do," Martin said. "Just let the officer know."

Andy nodded.

"Don't talk to anyone if you do," Martin said. "The media are vultures."

Andy followed Martin and Arthur as they walked into the hall, taking the first left into the kitchen. He looked down at the body of the dog, unable to make out the breed. A puddle of blood formed, soaking through the towel.

The police officer, average height and toned, with tattoo sleeves on both arms, tapped Andy on the shoulder.

"He didn't suffer mate," The police officer said. "It was quick."

"What kind is it?" Andy asked curiously.

"Border collie I think," the officer said. "Never seen one behave like it."

"Probably scared," Andy said, looking towards the kitchen.

"It's nasty in there," The officer said. "Hope you didn't have a big breakfast."

"Any relatives?" Martin asked the officer, who shook his head.

"She lost her husband a few years ago," He said. "Spoke to the neighbours, no other family apparently, however, she has a nephew in New Zealand."

"Poor old girl," Arthur said.

Arther and Martin walked in first, looking at the scene before them. The smell hit Andy before he had a chance to walk into the kitchen, the mask made no difference.

"Wow," Andy groaned.

It was worse than chicken or anything he had smelt, mingled with the dog's excrement and urine.

"Jesus," Andy said, his hand going to his nose.

The kitchen spanned the length of the house, under the window at the front, is a large ceramic sink with a double draining board, either side underneath is a washing machine and a dishwasher. A white worktop and pine cupboards run the length of the kitchen, with a double refrigerator covered in various fridge magnets humming away at the end. At the opposite end of the kitchen is a pine kitchen table with four matching chairs around it, a door leading to the living room, and a chest freezer under the long window. The worktop has several shopping bags, filled with items laid out, some had spilt to the floor, the packets torn and chewed. The light grey tiles were littered with food, packaging, and bloody paw prints.

The body of the elderly lady was face down, not far from the sink. Her head at an awkward angle, resting against the twelve-pack of dog food, dried blood pooled around it. Dressed in a black skirt and a floral blue blouse, the skirt has been pulled up, revealing her buttocks and thighs.

"That is nasty," Andy said, his face screwed up in disgust.

Parts of the woman's buttocks and thighs had been torn away, and blood splattered around the body. Flies are buzzing around and maggots crawling in the wounds.

"Poor old girl," Arthur said. "We are going to need some help."

"I can help," Andy said.

"You sure?" Martin asked. "It's not nice."

"It's okay," Andy said. "I need to do this."

Arthur looked at Martin, shrugging his shoulders and nodding.

"Okay," Martin said. "Could you unzip the body bag and lay it out," Martin said. "Over there. "He pointed to a clear spot on the kitchen floor. "Mind the dog crap."

Arthur handed the folded body bag to Andy, watching as Andy carefully laid it out on the floor and unzipped it, as close to the body as he could. Martin and Arthur took out latex gloves from their pockets, doubling up on them.

"We always use two sets," Arthur said. "Just in case."

"I am going to wait outside," The officer said. "I need the air." Martin nodded as the officer walked away, looking at Arthur and shaking his head.

"Ready?" Martin said to Arthur. "You get the legs."

"Sure?" Arthur asked. "I don't mind getting that end."

"No," Martin said. "Roll her onto her back first and then lift her onto the bag," He said. "Good?"

"Good with me," Arthur said and bent down, pulling the woman's skirt down, covering her buttocks and legs. He took hold of her ankles. "On three," Arthur said to Martin who nodded. "One, two and Three!"

They rolled the body onto its back and it let out a gurgle, like a plug being pulled in a bath.

"What was that?" Andy asked curiously, looking around.

"The body," Arthur said. "Body fluids sloshing around."

"Oh lovely," Andy said looking around.

The woman's face is distorted and bloody, the packaging of the dog food had imprinted on her face, the plastic leaving deep creases. Her short curly grey hair was matted with blood on one side.

"Ready?" Martin asked.

"Yes," Arthur said.

Martin grunted as he lifted the woman from under her arms, Arthur holding her by the ankles as he stood up, moving her gently over to the body bag.

"Pull the bag towards me," Martin said to Andy.

"What?" Andy said. "Cannot lipread you."

"Move the bag towards me," Martin shouted.

Andy stepped closer, pulling down Martins's mask.

"Oh Jesus Chris!" He groaned. "I said can you pull the bag towards me."

Putting the mask back up, Andy then pulled the bag closer until Martin nodded in agreement. They lowered the body, carefully manoeuvring the arms and legs.

"What happens with the dog?" Andy asked.

"The vet will probably organise something," Arthur pulled down his mask. "Seeing as she has no next of kin here."

"Poor thing," Andy said.

"What about the poor old girl?" Martin said, pointing to her.

"I am more of a dog person," Andy scoffed.

Martin pulled the body bag over her, lining it up as Arthur zipped it up, moving the woman's dress out of the way.

"Hello?" A woman's voice echoed.

"What?" Andy said in confusion, looking at the bag.

"That came from behind you," Martin said. "Who is it?" Martin called out.

A woman, tall and slim wearing a suit appeared at the door, her hand covering her mouth.

84

"What on earth happened here?" She said looking around.

"You shouldn't be in here," Martin said. "You need to speak to the police officer."

"I live two doors down," She said. "I used to be the nurse for her husband," She said looking at the body bag. "Is she?"

"I am afraid so," Martin said. "She has been dead a while."

"I have been away," The woman said. "Travelling for work."

"Were you close?" Arthur asked.

"Yes," She said, tears welling in her eyes. "She used to babysit my daughter."

"Sorry for your loss," Arthur said. "But you really need to wait outside."

"Can I see her?" The woman asked, looking around at the mess in the kitchen. "She was so tidy," She said. "She would have hated this."

"I think the mess would be the least of her worries," Arthur said.

"It's not a good idea to see her in this state," Martin said. "Especially with the dog and everything."

"The dog?" She said. "What happened to the dog?"

Martin looked at Arthur, but before he could respond.

"The police shot it," Andy said.

"What?!" The woman exclaimed.

Arthur looked at Andy, shaking his head as to warn him not to say anything.

"You need to speak to the officer," Martin said. "We are not allowed to say anything, sorry."

"Fine," The woman said. "But I want to see her before I leave."

"Just show her," Arthur said.

Martin unzipped the bag, pulling it back to reveal the old woman's face.

"Oh my god," The woman moaned. "Poor Elsie!"

"I am sorry for your loss," Martin said, pulling the bag back and zipping it up.

The woman groaned, the colour draining from her face.

"She is going," Arthur said and got to his feet, but he wasn't quick enough.

The woman fainted, falling backwards, and slamming into the wall behind her, she then slid down onto her side, her face inches away from a large pile of excrement.

"Go and get the officer for me, Andy," Martin said. "Come and give me a hand Arthur."

And stepped over the woman, trying not to laugh as he made his way outside, pulling off the mask.

Andy sat in the staffroom, with a newspaper, sandwich, and a bottle of water. A large fan is in the middle of the room, oscillating towards the table.

The door opened and Leanne walked in, wearing a short black skirt and white blouse.

"My god!" She moaned. "It's so hot!"

"It is," Andy said. "Really stuffy!"

"How are you doing?" She said as she approached the sink, filling up a water bottle. "Heard you had an exciting run this morning."

"Yeah," Andy smiled. "It was an interesting one."

"The police took the woman to hospital," Leanne said. "She had to have the cut on her head glued."

"She had a bit of a fright," Andy said. "She worked in Accident and Emergency for years, so not sure why she was so freaked out."

"Probably different when it's someone you know," Leanne said. "I saw my grandmother the day she died, and I was a wreck."

"Sorry to hear that," Andy said. "How did she die?"

"Fell out of the bloody loft!" Leanne scoffed. "She was hiding cigarettes!"

"Bet she never thought they would kill her," Andy said. "In that sense."

"I like that," Leanne chuckled. "That is funny."

"How's your day going?" Andy asked.

"The air conditioner has broken down in the office," She huffed. "So it's bloody warm."

"Sounds painful," Andy said. "I hate the heat."

Leanne drank half of the bottle of water, sighing in relief.

"Are you sure you are okay," She said. "Today not bother you?"

"No," Andy said. "Not as bad as I thought it would be, just the smell and the dog."

"Martin told me about the dog," She whined. "That was really sad."

"Yeah," Andy said. "What is the worst thing you have seen?" Andy asked. "Have you been on collections?"

"Only a couple," She said. "Hopefully never again, not my thing."

"Seen any bad ones?" Andy asked.

"Well they are all bad really," She said with a smile. "Where death is concerned."

"You know what I mean," Andy said. "Come on spill."

"It was a collection from the hospital," Leanne sighed heavily, sadness in her voice. "A little boy that had died from cancer."

"Oh shit that is bad," Andy said. "Sorry."

"The funeral was really nice," She smiled. "He loved red, so practically everything was red, even our hubcaps."

"That is cool," Andy said.

"Yeah," She took a deep breath. "What have the old sods got you doing?"

"Well I am waiting on Arthur or Martin to let me know," Andy said. "Although I heard Martin attended a funeral and Arthur is doing the ash collection."

"Yes," She said. "I would invite you upstairs, but trust me," She shook her head. "It isn't fun up there with the heat, or Marcia."

"Is she that bad?" Andy asked curiously.

"No," Leanne chuckled softly. "She is a really nice person, but dedicated and takes no shit."

"Only met her twice," Andy said. "She seems okay with me."

"How long have you lived at the boarding school," Leanne said, sipping at the water. "Martin told me you go to the school for the deaf."

"Yeah," Andy said. "Been there for three years now."

"How is it?" Leanne asked. "Do you enjoy it?"

"Not particularly," Andy said. "But as long as I read or go for walks in my free time, it's okay."

"Miss your parents?" She asked. "Sorry if I am nosey, it's a female thing."

"It's fine," Andy said. "Nice to be able to talk to someone, and no," He shook his head. "I don't."

"Not close?" Leanne said. "Sorry to hear that."

"It's okay," Andy said. "My mother wasn't keen on boys and reminded me regularly."

"Sorry, that sucks," Leanne said. "My dad wanted a son but got me."

"Switch?" Andy said.

Leanne laughed, turned around and filled up the bottle again. The door opened and Arthur walked in, pausing when he saw Leanne.

"You hiding from Marcia again?" Arthur asked. "You need a new hiding spot.

"It's so bloody hot," Leanne complained.

"All you office geeks have your air conditioning up there," He laughed. "What is the problem?"

"It's on the blink," Leanne rolled her eyes.

"Again," Arthur said. "Every year that thing breaks down, and probably needs servicing."

"It's just been serviced," Leanne said.

"Convenient," Arthur said. "I'll have a look at it later for you."

"Thanks, Art," Leanne smiled. "I'll get you some jellybeans." Leanne walked up to Arthur, kissing him on the cheek.

"Careful," He said. "You will make the kid jealous."

"Not a chance," Andy said. "Too hot for all that fuss."

"You might be right there," Leanne said. "Back to the hotplate!" She said in frustration and opened the door, poking her tongue out at Arthur before leaving.

"You good?" He asked Andy, sitting in the seat opposite.

"Fine," Andy said. "Anything exciting happening?" he asked curiously, hoping for something to do.

"No," Arthur said. "It's a quiet afternoon, you can always go if you want?"

"Is there anything that needs doing?" Andy asked. "Anything?"

"Let me have a think," He said. "There is something but it's boring," He said.

"I don't mind," Andy replied. "I am bored!"

"The cold store needs cleaning," He said. "It's done every day, but we have no collections due so it can be done earlier."

"I'll take it," Andy said. "It's the coolest room in the building!" Arthur laughed knowingly.

"You okay to do it on your own?" He asked. "You helped yesterday didn't you?"

"Yes," Andy said. "Keep me busy for an hour or two."

"Good lad," He said. "You know where everything is?"

"Yes," Andy said. "Do you want the spare trolley cleaned too?"

"Go for it," Artur said. "It's in the hall."

"The one with the squeaky wheel?" Andy laughed.

"That is the one," Arthur said. "Maybe you can get it to stop squeaking?"

Andy had been in the cold storage for half an hour, he had wiped down the storage units and had both the trolleys in the room.

"Right," Andy said. "Let's see how heavy this is."

Andy tipped the trolley slowly on the side, the weight of it nearly pulling him over as he brought it down, resting it on his toes, groaning as it pinched him.

"Jesus!" He scoffed. "Heavy!"

"Hello!" A voice said.

Andy froze and then turned around, looking in the doorway.

"Someone there?" Andy said.

"It's cold!" The voice again.

Andy walked over to the doorway, looking down the corridor.

"Someone there?" He said loudly.

No answer.

Andy then looked through the door into the courtyard that led to the coffin workshop, a converted barn.

"Someone say something?" Andy asked again.

He returned to the cold storage, noticing a handprint on the side of the refrigeration unit.

"That needs a good clean," He said to himself and returned to cleaning the trolley.

Looking closely at the wheels, he noticed the hair built up around one of them, restricting it from moving freely.

"I think I have the culprit," He tapped it. "Wonder if they have any spanners?"

"Hello!" A voice came again and Andy suddenly turned around in fright, knocking the trolley.

The trolley flipped over with a loud echoing clang and Andy flinched, pausing, and watching the door, his face screwed up in worry.

After a few minutes, he heard the echoing footsteps getting closer until Arthur appeared in the doorway.

"What on earth are you doing?" he asked. "I felt that down the corridor!"

"Sorry," Andy said. "I was cleaning the wheels."

"Well you are dedicated," Arthur laughed softly. "Didn't hurt yourself did you?"

"No," Andy replied. "Got distracted by voices."

"Voices?" Arthur said looking around curiously. "There is no one about, so do you mean the ones in your head kid?"

"Ha bloody ha," Andy rolled my eyes. "No, I could hear someone saying hello."

"Right," Arthur said listening briefly. "Well everyone in here is dead," He nodded, well we only have four bodies and trust me, they are very dead."

"Can you lend a hand?" Andy pointed to the trolley. "It's awkward."

Arthur helped Andy turn the trolley back onto its side, noticing the wheel.

"That probably explains the squeak," Arthur said looking closer. "Let me go get some tools."

Andy watched Arthur leave the room, heading towards the coffin store. He leaned against the refrigeration unit, gasping as the cold metal touched the back of his forearms.

"Hello?" the voice again. "Is anyone there."

"What?" Andy said. "Who said that?"

"What is going on?" Marcia said appearing at the door.

Marcia is short and slim, wearing dark grey trousers and a white blouse. Her hair was combed back into a ponytail and grey, almost silver under the harsh light. She has silver-rimmed glasses, hanging from her neck on a strap.

"Hi Marcia," Andy said. "I was cleaning and accidentally knocked over the trolley."

"Sounded like a bomb went off," Marcia chuckled. "Are you okay?"

"I am fine thanks," Andy said. "Arthur is getting some tools, we have found the cause of the squeak."

"Brilliant," She said. "That has annoyed people for years," She smiled. "How is the work experience treating you, I hear you had a very eventful day."

"It was interesting," Andy said. "I am enjoying it."

"Martin has updated me," She said. "Gerald and Arthur have been singing your praise, appears you are very keen."

"I like to keep busy," Andy said.

"Did you offer to clean this room due to it being the coolest room in the building?" She said. "No one ever volunteers to clean."

"It was better than sitting in the staffroom," Andy said. "Out of the frying pan and into the freezer!"

Arthur walked into the room, almost bumping into Marcia.

"Come to tell him off for making a racket?" Arthur laughed.

"No," Marcia said. "At least someone is doing some work today."

"Touche," Arthur said, altering the monkey wrenches. "Everything okay?"

"Yes," Marcia said. "Was just catching up with Andy about the placement," She said. "And thanks for sorting out the air con, what was it?"

"Filter," Arthur said. "It will switch off when it reaches a certain hour of use."

"But it was serviced recently?" She moaned. "I am going to complain."

"Don't blame you," Marcia said.

A cough caused Marica and Arthur to go quiet, looking towards the refrigeration unit.

94

"Either one of our bodies isn't quite dead," Marcia said. "Or someone is trying to prank Andy?"

Arthur shook his head.

"Sounded like it came from there," Arthur pointed to the compartment closest to the window and two up from the floor. "Who is in the building?" He asked.

"Just Leanne, you, Andy and myself," Marcia said. "Everyone else is out."

Marcia turned around when she heard footsteps and Leanne appeared at the doorway.

"I am going to pop out and get some ice cream," Leanne said with a smile. "You all want one?"

"Yes please," A voice came from the compartment.

"I think it would be an idea to call the police," Marcia said. "What do you think?" She said looking at Arthur.

"That sounds like Nick," Leanne said. "Is that you Nick?"

Laugher broke out and Arthur shook his head, walking over to the compartment and opening it.

Nick laid on the tray, average height, and build, he has short hair and a well-groomed goatee. He is wearing tanned boots, blue jeans, and a grey shirt.

"What are you doing?" Marica snapped. "This isn't a playground."

"I heard about the new kid," Nick said, pulling himself out of the compartment. "And couldn't resist pranking him with the voices."

"And there was me thinking he was winding me up," Arthur said. "Sorry, Andy."

"How long have you been in there you idiot?" Leanne asked.

"About half an hour," Nick said laughing. "He was a little slow to catch on, but it was funny."

"You are aware that Andy is deaf?" Marcia said.

"Deaf?" Nick said. "As in completely?"

"No not completely," Andy said. "I need to lipread with the use of sound and cannot locate sounds."

"You arsehole," Leanne said. "Who put you up to it?"

"No one," Nick said. "I was talking to Gerald yesterday and had the idea earlier."

"Should have left him in there," Macia said. "Anyhow I need to talk to you, we have two damaged coffins this week."

"I am on that," Nick said. "I think they are from the batch that fell off my lorry last week."

"Fell off the lorry?" Marcia scoffed. "How on earth did that happen?"

"The tail failed," Arthur said. "That is when we had to manually lift off fifteen standards."

"Were they not checked?" Marcia questioned Arthur.

"Yes," Arthur said. "But the cracks were not apparent until they had a body in them."

"Well it was lucky that Gerald noticed the crack before the funeral started, otherwise it would have been bedlam!" She said, anger in her voice. "We have a standard to keep."

"I think it's ice cream time," Leanne said.

"I agree," Marcia took a deep breath. "Use some petty cash, I will treat everyone."

"Me too?" Nick grinned mischievously.

"If I find you getting in those compartments again," Marica pointed a finger at him in warning. "I will lock you in there for the night."

"Sorry," Nick said. "I know you love me really."

"You are lucky you are my nephew," She said, trying not to smile.

"Nice to meet you, Andy," Nick said holding out his hand. "Sorry about that, no hard feelings."

"Tell you what," Arthur said. "Could you help Nick with the two coffins? I will finish the trolley and then you can help me flip it back up."

"Sure," Andy said.

"I am heading to Rottingdean after the ice cream," Nick said. "You go to that deaf school don't you?"

Andy nodded.

"I can drop you off," Nick said. "Save you having to get the bus?"

"I have a few hours yet," Andy said looking at his watch.

"It's fine," Marcia said. "You have done enough for us today, and I appreciate it, finish after we have had our ice cream."

"Okay thanks," Andy said. "I could do with a cold shower."

"I think we all could," Leanne said. "It's so hot and sticky!"

"Go and get our ice cream then," Marcia said. "Get a couple of boxes of choc ices, stick them in the freezer."

"Come on Andy," Nick said. "Hope you are feeling strong, my tail lift is still buggered!"

# WEDNESDAY

On either side of the large room are various designs of coffins, three mounted on the wall perfectly in line with each other. A display cabinet with urns, plagues and bibles is at the centre of the room. The blood red carpet is clean, the walls in magnolia and the ceilings pure white, the warm glow from the three-bulb lighting at the centre. Behind the couch are two doors, one leading to a waiting room, and another leading to a hall to the rest of the building. On both sides of the doors, are large golden framed mirrors, clean and polished.

Andy is vacuuming around the edges of the urn display cabinet when the hoover cuts out, he turns round and notices the electrical plug has come out of the socket.

"Bloody hell," He mumbles, walking over to it.

The door opens and Martin walks in, looking around.

"You started yet?" He asks with a mischievous smile.

"What?" Andy looks up.

"Have you started yet?" Martin asked again.

"Funny," Andy grins. "You doing any work today?"

"Yes," Martin laughs softly. "Have you seen Arthur?"

"He is getting the viewing ready," Andy said. "Asked me to give the place a hoover."

"Strange," Martin said. "It was done last night."

"A delivery came in and they unpacked it in here," Andy said. "polystyrene everywhere."

"Oh you are joking!" Martin scoffed. "Bloody couriers!"

"Just got a little bit more to do," Andy said. "Then done."

"Brilliant," Martin said. "It's great having you here."

"Can I have that in writing?" Andy asked.

"No," Martin said, making his way towards the back door. "Get on with it!"

"Mean," Andy moaned.

"The viewing will be here soon," Martin said. "Could you make sure the cable isn't running across the room."

"Sure," Andy said. "Pretty much done."

Martin gave Andy a thumbs up and left the room, gently closing the door behind him.

Andy pushed the plug back in and the vacuum burst into life, he walked over to it picked it back up and turned it off. As he looked out of the window, one of the coffins caught his attention.

"That looks odd," Andy said and walked over to it.

The middle-mounted coffin is leaning down, almost resting on the one below. He looked at the bracket, noticing it was coming away from the wall.

"Wonder if they know about this?" Andy said softly to himself.

The bracket came away from the wall slightly and the coffin dropped, resting against the third coffin below it with a clunk, Andy flinched, his hand reaching out as if he were to catch it.

"Shit," Andy said. "Better let Arthur know.

The door to the waiting room opened and Arthur walked in, sighing heavily.

"My!" He groaned. "It's warm this morning," He looked around. "Done a good job."

There is a tap on the door and Arthur turned, looking at the tall heavily built man, his large frame almost filling the whole doorway.

"Hello?" Arthur said. "Can I help you?"

The door opened and the man, wearing a black three-piece suit walked in, closing it gently behind him.

"Hi," He said. "Arthur is it?"

"Oh yes," Arthur said holding out his hand. "We did your father's funeral."

"Father-in-law," The man said smiling.

"Sorry," Arthur said apologetically. "How can I help?"

"My wife asked me to collect the bits," He said.

"What bits?" Arthur asked. "I am not aware of any bits?" He looked at Andy.

"Don't look at me," Andy shook his head.

"Remind me," Arthur said. "What is it you are collecting?"

"The shoes and the waistcoat," The man said. "My wife brought them in for him to wear."

"That your father-in-law was wearing?" Arthur said. The man nodded.

"Did you ask for them to be returned?" Arthur asked. "I didn't see anything on the notes."

"No idea," The man said.

"Okay," Arthur sighed. "It would have been asked if anything needed to be retrieved before the cremation."

"Oh!" The man exclaimed. "Has he been cremated already?" Arthur nodded.

"When?" The man asked.

"On the same day," Athur added. "In the evening most likely."

"Well shit," The man said. "My wife bought them for my birthday when we met."

"I can suggest either telling her the truth," Arthur nodded. "Or try and find replacements."

"Are you sure that they are definitely gone?" The man said. "Like very sure?"

"Cremation tends to leave nothing behind," Arthur said. "Only ash."

"Shit," The man said, taking a deep breath. "Better let the wife know the bad news!"

The man smiled unsurely, and then walked to the door, pausing and then leaving.

Arthur looked at the door as it closed, and then back at Andy, chuckling softly.

"So where were we?" Arthur said. "Brain like a sieve."

"Have you seen the coffin display?" Andy said, just as the door opened.

A woman walked in, short and petite wearing a white blouse, black skirt, and black heels. Her long black hair is tied back neatly into a ponytail. She holds a small black briefcase under her arm.

"Hello there," Arthur said. "Mrs Turner?"

Mrs Turner nodded, her eyes red from crying.

"Would you like to come into the waiting room?" Arther pointed.

"Could I wait a bit," She said. "My brother will be here soon."

"Of course," Arthur said. "Would you like a drink?"

"Could I have water?" She said softly. "Please?"

"Sure," Arthur smiled. "Will go and grab that for you."

Andy rolled up the lead for the hoover, carrying it over to the corner of the room and putting it down. Struggling with the hose, a mind of its own as it flops and flaps around.

"May I sit down?" Mrs Turner asks Andy, pointing to the couch. Andy didn't respond, walking past the woman and checking around the cabinet.

"Excuse me," Mrs Turner said. "Can you hear me?"

"Sorry?" Andy said. "What was that?"

"Can I sit down?" She asked again, confusion on her face.

"Of course," Andy said Smiling. "Sorry," He pointed to his ears. "I am deaf."

"Oh I am sorry," Mrs turner raised her voice.

"It's okay," Andy replied. "Just speak normally."

"I did," She said. "You didn't hear me."

"Sorry," Andy said.

The woman sat down, holding the briefcase against her knees.

"How long have you worked here," She asked. "If you don't mind me asking."

"I don't work here," Andy said. "Work experience."

"Oh," Mrs Turner said curiously.

103

"This is my third day," Andy said. "Really enjoying it, meeting tons of people."

"Really," she nodded nervously. "What are you doing?" She said. "When you leave school?"

"Acting," Andy said. "I want to go into performing arts."

"My brother does that," She said. "On cruise ships."

"Oh wow," Andy nodded in interest. "I bet that is so much fun."

"He loves it," She said. "Just that we don't get to see him much." Andy didn't know what else to say, he smiled awkwardly, slowly looking around the room.

"Your water should be along soon," Andy said.

"It has been ever so hot," She took a deep breath and blew out slowly. "I am not a fan of the heat."

"Neither am I," Andy said. "I think it's going to rain later," He smiled. "Should cool things down a little."

"Is it hot where you work?" The woman asked. Andy thought about the cold storage, how ice cool it was and he would go there and cool down, but his head was telling him not to talk about it, considering her father had just been brought back from there.

"Very," Andy said. "But lots of water helps, and shade," He said. "The barn is quite cool."

"What do they keep in there?" She asked curiously.

"Oh," Andy paused. "It's for the cars," He lied. "We keep all the cleaning stuff in there."

"Okay," She nodded, looking through the window.

"So what brings you here?" Andy said, then realising the stupidity of the question he asked and took a deep breath. "Sorry, that was a stupid question."

"No it's okay," She said. "It's my father," Her voice broke, "He died."

"I am sorry for your loss," Andy said.

"Cancer took him," She coughed, covering her mouth briefly. "He died at home, surrounded by family."

"That is the main thing," Andy said. "Being with family."

The woman started to cry, her hands going to her face as the sobs racked her.

"Sorry," Andy said. "Did I upset you."

"No!" She sobbed, shaking her head. "I just cannot believe he is gone."

Andy walked over to the couch, looking towards the door, wondering where Arthur had got to.

"Can I get you anything?" Andy said feeling awkward.

The woman stood up, grabbing hold of Andy, and hugging him, her sobs becoming louder. Andy stood still, his hands at his sides as he was unsure what to do with them.

"I am sorry!" She cried. "I am so stupid."

Andy didn't respond, he couldn't understand what she was saying, her mouth covered and her words muffled amongst the crying.

The door opened and Arthur appeared, holding a bottle of water and a brown envelope.

"What is going on?" He said silently.

Andy shook his head.

"Are you okay there Mrs Turner?" Arthur said. "I have your water."

"I am sorry," She broke away from Andy, noticing the slight makeup on his shoulder. "Sorry about that!" She said.

"It's okay," Andy said. "Nothing to be sorry for."

She sat back down, reaching for the water bottle as Arthur handed it to her.

"We just had a call," Arthur said. "Your brother is delayed, traffic," Arthur sighed. "He said to go ahead without him if you want to?"

"I cannot do it alone," She cried. "I can't."

"You won't be alone," Arthur said. "I will come in with you, or even Andy. If you prefer we do have a female that can assist."

"Would that be okay?" She said. "I don't want to be any trouble."

"That would be perfectly okay," Arthur said. "let me go and get her."

"Thank you," She sobbed. "I appreciate it."

"Keep her company for a few minutes please," Arthur said and left the room.

"I am sorry," She forced a smile. "You must think I am stupid."

"No," Andy said. "Not at all, I do understand."

"Have you lost anyone?" She asked.

Andy nodded slowly.

"Yes," He said. "My uncle passed away this year," Andy took a deep breath. "He was like a father to me, taught me so much and believed in me."

"Sorry to hear that," She said. "Did you see him?"

"No," Andy shook his head.

"Did you want to?" She asked.

"No," Andy said. "I wanted to remember him how he was."

"I didn't see my father the day he died," She said, smiling. "I saw him the night before, and we talked for an hour," She chuckled. "I had my dad back for that hour, and I felt like his little girl."

"That is sweet," Andy said. "Those moments are amazing."

"He died the next day," She said, her smile disappearing. "I was late, due to a meeting and when I got there, he had already died."

"It's sad, but it happens," Andy said. "You had that hour with him though, that is something."

"That is true," She said.

The door opened and Arthur walked in, followed by Leanne who was wearing a black skirt and a white blouse. Her hair is shorter, cropped at the shoulders and highlighted.

"This is Leanne," Arthur said. "She will take you to the viewing once you are ready."

"Thank you," Mrs Turner said. "I am being really silly, you must think I am stupid."

"Not at all!" Arthur said. "These things are never nice, and we have all been there."

"Would you like anything before you go in?" Leanne asked her.

"No," She said. "Can I have a minute?"

"Of course," Leanne said. "Everything okay Andy?" She asked with a smile.

"Yes," Andy said. "Hair looks nice."

"I only just noticed," Arthur scoffed.

"Well at least someone did!" She said. "Blokes in this place!"

"I noticed!" Andy said.

Arthur laughed.

"I see you got this place looking nice and tidy," Leanne walked around. "I have no idea what that courier was playing at."

"Oh that reminds me," Andy said. "Arthur did you know that...." Before Andy could finish his sentence, the door opened and a tall slim man walked in, wearing a white t-shirt, blue jeans, and brown boots. He has long light brown hair down to his shoulders, messy and greasy.

"I thought you were delayed!" Mrs Turner said, jumping to her feet and running over to him, hugging him, and crying.

"Sorry," He said. "I parked the car and ran the rest of the way, bloody traffic man!"

"It's all good," Arthur said.

"Close the door," She said. "Let's go and see dad."

The man slammed the door closed, and at this moment there is a large scrape followed by a hollow thump. The second coffin falls from the mountings, taking the bottom one with it and rolling into the middle of the floor, the lid flipping off.

"Shit!" The man said.

The top coffin then fell heavily to the ground, the wood splintering as it broke in half, the lid popping off and landing at Andy's feet. Mrs Turner yelped and jumped back, looking around in confusion, her mouth open in shock.

"Jesus," The man said. "I always thought they had bodies in them."

Arthur and Leanne looked at the man.

"You are thick sometimes," Mrs Turner said. "They are for show."

"Well, I know that now!" The man said. "This place haunted or something?" He asked. "I mean you do get a lot of dead bodies in here don't you?"

"It's a funeral parlour," Andy said. "There is your clue."

"Bloody hell," She said. "You are an idiot," She gently shoved the man. "Why did you have to slam the door?"

"Don't worry," Leanne said. "It's no one's fault, shall we go into the waiting room?"

Mrs Turner nodded and Leanne led them into the waiting room, holding the door open as they both walked in, rolling her eyes at Arthur as she closed the door.

"That is what I wanted to say," Andy said. "Bracket looked a bit iffy."

"Sorry Andy," Arthur said.

Arthur started laughing, his hand over his mouth trying to stifle them.

"Did you see the look on their faces?" Andy said. "I didn't know if she was going to laugh or cry."

"Fancy helping me clear the mess up?" Arthur asked. "We can put them in the hall and I will get Nick to put the brackets up."

"Sure," Andy said. "The bottom one looks like it survived the fall."

"They are pretty solid," Arthur said nodding in appreciation. "And expensive."

"I bet," Andy said. "Do they cremate in those?"

"No," Arthur said. "They are purely for burial, no one would spend that kind of money just to set it on fire."

"You would be surprised," Andy said. "There are millions that spend a fortune on cigarettes."

"Good point," Arthur chuckled. "After that, I need some help in the workshop if you are feeling creative?" Arthur said. "After some breakfast obviously!"

Andy grunted as he lowered the large rectangular coffin onto the floor, bending his knees and looking at Arthur who is red in the face. They both stood in the corridor leading to the cold store and barn. All three coffins had been moved into the corridor and laid out. The largest was undamaged, other than a dent in the corner, hardly noticeable.

"I am not as strong as I used to be Andy," Arthur is breathing heavily, groaning as he stretches. "These things weigh a ton."

"Should we have taken the bricks out first?" Andy scoffed, trying not to laugh.

"You have a point," Arthur said. "Fancy winding up Martin?"

"How?" Andy asked.

Arthur pointed to the coffin.

"What?" Andy said, unsure what Arthur was getting at.

"Hide in the coffin," Arthur said.

"Me?" Andy said curiously. "Is this another attempt at a prank?"

"Would I do that?" Arthur said innocently.

"Yes," Andy nodded.

"Come on," Arthur said. "Get in there and hide," Arthur grinned. "I want to see him jump!"

"Okay," Andy said unsure. "Not going to leave me in there are you?"

"Would I?" Arthur said. "Would I do that?"

Andy shrugged his shoulders.

"Go on," Arthur said, opening up the lid of the pine, decorated coffin. The inside is decorated with cushioned cream fabric, a pillow at the head with a cross on it in red.

"Bloody cross!" Andy yelped. "I am going to burst into flames!"

"Oh you will be fine," Arthur said. "To nice to be the son of the devil."

"You would be surprised," Andy said as he carefully climbed into the coffin, lowering himself down and lying flat. "This is actually pretty comfortable."

"Good," Arthur said. "Keep quiet until I call you," Arthur paused. "Will you hear?"

"Should do," Andy nodded.

"Good," Arthur said, closing the coffin lid.

As it slowly closed, Andy heard the click. He lay in the darkness, thinking and trying not to laugh, the odd giggle escaping from him. Minutes passed and he started to get hot and uncomfortable, the air becoming thin and stuffy.

"I need air," Andy said and pushed against the lid.

The lid failed to open.

"What the fuck?" Andy said, slight worry in his voice.

He pushed it again, harder.

"What is going on?" Andy muttered to himself. "Feels like something against the top."

He went quiet when he heard a noise.

"Can you hear that?" Leanne said. "Sounds like scratching."

"I hope it's not rats again!" She moaned. "Those bloody bins next door are always overflowing."

He listened for a while, as best as he could and then he heard his name. He pushed against the lid as hard as he could and it flipped open, slamming against the wall.

Marcia and Leanne screamed out in fright, jumping back from the coffin.

"Jesus!" Marcia yelped.

Leanne burst into hysterics, unable to talk.

"You little shit!" Marcia snapped, trying not to laugh. "Which arse put you up to this."

"I am not sure I should say," Andy said.

"I will buy you lunch," Marcia said. "Come on."

"I was supposed to be pranking Martin," Andy said.

"Arthur put you up to this?" She asked.

Andy nodded.

"Knew it," Leanne said. "Every bloody time!"

"Let's switch," Marcia said. "Go and stand behind the door," She pointed. "Quickly!"

"What do you want me to do?" Leanne said smiling.

"When he comes in, knock on the coffin," She giggled. "Gonna wind up the old git."

Andy climbed out and hid behind the door as Marcia climbed into the coffin, lowering the lid.

"There is a latch on the side," She pointed. "Just so you know."

"Could have done with that information before I got in," Andy said. "Like a bloody oven."

"Language!" Marcia warned him and closed the lid.

Leanne walked towards the door as it opened.

"There you are," Arthur said. "Where is Martin?"

"Popped out," Leanne said. "Can I help?"

"Actually you can," Arthur said grinning. "Could you open the coffin for me?"

"Why?" Leanne asked curiously.

"The latch is stuck," Arthur said. "I cannot seem to unlatch it, and I know you have a knack."

"Fine," Leanne rolled her eyes and bent down, knocking on the coffin twice. "Anyone in there?"

Two knocks came from the coffin.

"That is creepy," Leanne said looking at Arthur who is trying not to laugh. "Who is in there?" She knocked three times.

Three knocks came from the coffin.

"Wonder who it is?" She said. "Maybe it's Andy?" Leanne gasped.

"Not me," Andy said from the corner.

Arthur looked at him in confusion, and then at the coffin in worry.

"Hello Andy," Leane said. "Is there a body in here?"

"Not as far as I know," Andy said shaking his head and looking at Arthur.

"Who is in there?" Arthur asked Andy silently.

Andy shrugged his shoulders.

There is a click and the coffin lid slowly opens.

"Oh shit," Arthur said. "It's Countess Marcia."

She sat up, looking at Arthur with one eyebrow raised.

"Did you try to get Andy to scare the crap out of me?" She asked.

"No not you," Arthur said. "Trying to get my own back on Martin."

"You could have told the poor sod where the latch was," Leanne said. "He was boiling in there!"

"You set me up?" Arthur looked at Andy who shook his head innocently.

"We came in here for a private chat," Leanne sniggered. "Got a bit worried when we heard noises coming from the coffin."

"I thought we had rats again!" Marica said, climbing out of the coffin awkwardly until Arthur reached out, helping her.

"Rats?" Andy said.

"Yeah," Arthur said. "Next door had overflowing bins, ended up having rats running in."

"Lovely," Andy said. "Reminds me of a certain horror book!"

"Oh you read?" Leanne said curiously.

"I do," Andy said. "You?"

"Horror all the way mate!" She smiled. "Love it."
Marica looked at the coffin.

"Is this the one that fell off the wall?" She asked.

"Yes, but it was one from the bottom," Arthur said. "Minor scuff but no damage, the other two need repair or scrapping."

"Did the customers complain?" Marcia asked. "From the viewing?"

"In fact no," Leanne said. "Once I got them into the waiting room, they both burst into fits of laughter, apparently their father would have loved it."

"Well that is god," Marcia said. "You got things to do?" She looked at Arthur.

"Yes," Arthur said. "I am sorting out the display after I have some food, and Andy here is helping out Gerald."

"How are you finding it with us Andy?" Marica asked.

"Really enjoying it," Andy said. "Apart from the hug earlier this morning," He pulled a disgusted face. "Wasn't too keen on that."

"Who hugged you?" Marcia said, looking at Leanne and then Arthur.

"Wasn't me!" Arthur exclaimed. "Was the customer, the woman from this morning."

"She caught me by surprise," Andy said. "Thought she was after my wallet!"

"Funny," Marcia shook her head. "I heard you handled it well down there, if you like you can sit in with Leanne the next time a funeral is booked?"

"That would be interesting," Andy said. "Thanks."

"Not a problem," Marcia said. "I am getting some sandwiches in for lunch, so will go and order those now."

"Go do some work old man," Leanne shoved Arthur playfully.

"See the abuse I put up with," Arthur shook his head. "Bloody heartbreaking."

"His wife tells us to," Leanne said.

"I believe you," Arthur said. "I really do."

The converted barn has two levels, the original wood building with parts updated and patched up with new wood. The inside has been recently renovated, with wooden panels and plasterboard. The ground floor is the workshop and generic coffin storage and the first floor is for the more expensive, rarely used coffins and various other supplies. From the double door entrance, is a doorway leading into the workshop, on the right are stairs leading to the first floor and a manual lift next to the stairs, a large sign indicating it is out of order. On the right is the workshop, two large workbenches with various tools covering them, the benches are old and worn.

In front of the bench, are racks for placing coffins on, four of them lined up, two per coffin. Only one has a coffin mounted on it, pine with white frilly material fitted internally. The plastic handles and fixtures glinted in the harsh fluorescent lights that ran down the middle of the workshop. At the far end of the workshop, are two large barn doors, bolted in several places with twenty-plus coffins piled up in front of them, against the wall near the stairs are smaller coffins and also cardboard coffins, flat packed.

Andy is stapling the material around the coffin edges, taking care, and concentrating. Gerald is nearby, leaning against the bench, watching him. A large floor fan is blowing on full, aimed in Andy's direction. The back of his shirt is wet with perspiration and he has blood on the back of his forearm.

"Is that okay?" Andy said looking up at Gerald.

"It's fine," Gerald said. "Carry on."

Andy continued to fit the skirting on the coffin, the staple gun snapping away.

Martin walked into the barn, groaning.

"How can you work in this heat?" He said. "Jesus Christ!"

"It is warm," Gerald said. "The fan helps a little and I tried to open the windows," He pointed to the long windows above the double doors. "But they won't open."

"How come?" Martin asked.

"The roller doesn't work," Gerald said. "I think someone must have overdone it at some point."

"Will get Nick to have a look," Martin said. "It was probably him that broke the bloody thing," He looked at Andy and then at the two coffins lined up nearby. "Did he do those?" Martin asked.

"Yes," Gerald said. "He did one with me on Monday but has done these himself."

Martin walked over to the coffins, inspecting them closely, nodding in admiration.

"Impressive," Martin said.

"He has a knack for it," Gerald said. "That way he can get on with it while I do other things."

"What have you been doing?" Martin asked.

"Sorted out the neonatal coffins," Gerald said. "And the cardboard, there has been a small leak by the back doors, so I have nicked a couple of pallets from the local supermarket and raised them off the floor," Gerald pointed into the corner. "Getting some more later to do the same with the generics."

"The roof needs checking too," Martin said. "Remember that storm last year?"

"Oh yes," Gerald laughed. "We had a bit of a storm that damaged the roof," He explained to Andy. "Water ran down over the Fusebox and blew it up."

"Bet that was a worry," Andy said.

"Marcia looked out the window and all she could see was smoke billowing out of the door," Martin scoffed. "She called the fire service but lucky for us, Nick was in with a fire extinguisher and put it out."

"I remember," Gerald replied. "The fire service were not happy."

"Remember that guy that kept double-checking if there were any bodies in there," Martin laughed. "Poor sod was petrified!" Martin noticed the blood on Andy's arm. "What have you done?"

"What?" Gerald said.

"Oh I did that earlier," Andy said. "It is only a scratch."

"Quite a bit of blood for a scratch," Martin said. "How did you do it?"

"One of the coffins had a sharp edge," Andy said. "Caught my arm as I lifted the coffin over."

"Wally," Gerald said, reaching for a first aid box on the bench and pulling out a pack of alcohol wipes. "Here," He said handing one to Andy. "That is going to sting."

Andy wiped the blood off his arm, hissing.

"Told you," Gerald laughed.

"How many left?" Martin said.

"One more after this," Gerald said. "He has completed the next two days."

"Bloody hell," Martin said. "He is more efficient than you are!"

"He taught me how to do them," Andy said. "So you could say he is efficient."

"You bribed him or something?" Martin looked at Gerald who shook his head innocently.

"Did you need something?" Gerald asked. "Or just getting in the way?"

"Would you be able to stand in for a viewing?" Martin asked.

"Sure," Gerald said. "I'll get things ready shortly."

Martin gave Gerald the thumbs up.

"Thanks," He said. "I appreciate it," He looked at Andy. "Did you know the workshop is haunted?" Martin said. "Ghosts of previous undertakers!"

"Sounds good," Andy said.

"Get back upstairs!" Gerald said and looked at Andy. "Let's get this one finished."

"Bloody rude," Martin moaned and laughed. "This is the way I get treated Andy."

"Brings it on himself," Gerald said.

"I do," Martin nodded as he left, closing the door behind him.

"What's happening with the coffin display?" Andy asked.

"We told Marcia it was your fault," Gerald said. "Told her you sat on one for a coffee break."

Andy looked at Gerald, mouth wide open in shock.

"Only kidding," Gerald laughed. "A kid pulled it down a couple of months ago."

"A kid?!" Andy exclaimed. "How the hell did they manage that?"

Gerald walked closer to Andy, picking up a bottle of water.

"The grandmother was in, booking a funeral for her sister," Gerald explained. "The kid was running around being mental as they do and decided to swing off it, the whole bloody thing came down on top of him!"

Andy burst out laughing, his hand going to his mouth as he slowly shook his head.

"Luckily he wasn't hurt," Gerald said. "Otherwise the grandmother would have been booking the second!"

"That is pretty bad," Andy said.

"The grandmother kicked off," Gerald sighed. "Laid into Martin like anything and wanted a discount for nearly killing her grandkid."

"Did she get it?" Andy said, groaning as he stretched his back.

"Not at all," Gerald scoffed. "Martin showed her the security footage, and she and her daughter ended up having a heated argument in the middle of the reception!"

"Mad," Andy shook his head. "Must have been fun."

"The fun started when Marcia came down and pretty much bashed their heads together," Gerald said. "She even offered them a discount to shut them up."

"So who put the bracket back up?" Andy said. "I can help with that if needed?"

"Nick did," Gerald said. "But the bracket wasn't broken, so over time constant door banging must have loosened it."

"I only noticed it when I was cleaning," Andy said. "Saw it move."

"Yeah, Arthur told me," Gerald said. "No idea why people slam that door so hard."

Andy paused, looking around when a rattling noise started, slowly becoming louder and heavier.

"What is that?" Andy asked.

"Rain," Gerald said. "Thin roof," He looked up. "Can you hear that then?"

"Oh yes," Andy scoffed. "Sounds like a tank rolling through!"

"It does get loud," Gerald said. "Used to be much worse when we had the old roof."

Andy put down the staple gun, yawning.

"Can I ask a question?" Andy said.

"Sure," Gerald nodded. "I will do my best to answer it."

"How come Martin doesn't drive the hearse or the limo?" Andy asked.

"Has he not told you?" Gerald said curiously. "That is unlike him not to brag."

Andy leaned against the wall, his arms crossed.

"Got a feeling it's going to be funny," Andy said, excitement in his voice.

"Not really no," Gerald said. "I haven't told you, but he was banned for a year."

"Bloody hell," Andy exclaimed. "What did he do?"

"Have a guess," Gerald said.

"Crash a hearse?" Andy guessed. "Am I close?"

The door opened and Arthur rushed in, groaning. His shirt and hair are slightly wet.

"Bloody coming down like hellfire out there!" Arthur snapped. "Jesus, a warning would have been nice!"

"Always complaining," Gerald rolled his eyes. "What do you want now?"

"I need your help," Arthur said. "If you are free, either one of you?"

"I will," Gerald said. "I need the toilet anyhow, but before I do, Andy here is guessing why Martin got banned for a year."

"Oh I have to hear this," Arthur chuckled.

"Speeding?" Andy said.

"Bloody good guess!" Arthur said. "First attempt?"

"Second," Gerald added. "He got clocked by police doing ninety on the motorway!" Gerald laughed. "Luckily there was nobody in the back, otherwise the shit would have hit the fan."

"He is lucky Marcia likes him," Arthur said. "Anyone else would have been sacked."

"Yeah," Gerald said. "Do you remember the guy we had that passed out at the steering wheel?

"Oh was this the war veterans' funeral?" Arthur said thinking. "When the relatives kicked off and we had to make up an excuse?"

"That is the one," Gerald smiled. "Basically Andy, we were about to leave the residence after loading all the florals, and one of our undertakers," He looked at Arthur. "What was his name?"

"Ahmed I think it was," Arther said. "Asian kid."

"Anyway," Gerald said. "We were just about to leave the house, with several veterans following the hearse to the end of the road, one of them had bagpipes and everything."

"Sounded like a cat being ripped to shreds," Arthur said bluntly. "I swear I lost some hearing that day."

"Shut up!" Gerald scoffed. "Ahmed passed out, face down in the steering wheel and set the horn off, the hearse rolled into a neighbour's car, scraping the side."

"Oh nasty!" Andy said.

"Marcia was there and everything, she was leading the funeral due to Martin being off," Gerald started laughing. "She got out when she realised something was wrong, opened the door and Ahmed fell out, mumbling and groaning about something."

"What happened to him?" Andy asked.

"Diabetic," Arthur said. "Never managed it properly, didn't declare it to us until that day."

"The pastries for breakfast didn't help," Gerald said. "After we ended up calling an ambulance for him twice, we had to let him go."

"I am surprised he wasn't sacked for damaging the hearse," Andy exclaimed. "Bloody hell!"

"Don't seem to have much luck with people," Arthur said.

"Obviously!" Andy said. "Like the guy that dropped the body in the cold room."

"Nightmare!" Gerald said. "All he was trying to do was make things easier but ended up making things ten times worse."

"Anyway," Arthur said. "You going to help me get the reception sorted?"

"Will you be okay while I pop out for a bit?" Gerald asked.

"Sure, I will be fine," Andy said confidently. "If I need anything, I will pop up to the office upstairs."

"Good lad," Gerald gave him a thumbs up. "Could you add two more to the list?"

"Same type?" Andy asked.

Gerald nodded and pointed to two coffins on a single pallet in front of the main stock.

"Those two," Gerald said. "Basic set up."

"Sure," Andy said. "No problems."

"Putting us all to shame you are!" Arthur chuckled. "Seriously though," He said. "We will be in reception, so give us a shout if you need anything."

"Will do," Andy picked up the staple gun.

"See you in a while," Gerald said, following Arthur as they left the barn, closing the door behind them.

Any had finished the last two coffins, stacking them on top of each other. He had cleared the workshop, sweeping up the mess and tidying up the tools.

"Strange," He said to himself. "He has been gone a while. Walking over to the doors, Andy pushed it, only to find it locked.

"Oh," Andy said. "That isn't right."

He tried again, pulling it in case it was jammed and then knocking several times, trying to get someone's attention.

"Hello?" He called out. "Anyone?"

No answer.

"Hello!" Andy called out. "I cannot open the door!"

Andy needed the toilet, he had put it off earlier, wanting to finish things.

"Telephone," Andy said. "I saw one earlier."

Noticing an old filing cabinet, he then saw the telephone on top of it.

"That should help," he said and picked up the phone, listening carefully but could not hear a dial tone. "Oh you are kidding!" He said pulling gently at the cable to find the wire had been ripped away from the wall. "Well, shit!"

He tried the door again, with no luck.

"At least I have a book," Andy said. "Suppose I could read a while until I wet myself!" He said in sarcasm.

He noticed the empty water bottle in the rubbish bin.

"Last resort," He said. "Better than wetting myself I guess."

An hour passed and Andy had checked all over the barn, looking for an alternative way out. He even climbed up to the double windows, to see if he could free them and climb out. He looked out into the courtyard, the rain coming down gently.

"Hello?!" He called out. "Anyone?"

No answer.

"Going to have to stay the night," Andy said. "That is going to be interesting, at least the coffins are comfortable."

Groaning in frustration, Andy walked over to the door, looking through the gap, noticing the door had been locked.

"Why is the door locked?" Andy scoffed. "Another bloody prank?"

Andy knocked on the door several times.

"Hello!" he called out, listening.

He walked back into the workshop, looking around.

"Cannot go the back way," He said. "Locked up," He looked at the ceiling. "Too high, cannot climb."

He noticed the water bottle.

"I really need a piss," He said to himself. "If I sneeze, I am going to wet myself!"

Andy hurried over to the bottle and took the cap off, undid the button on his trousers and

head the door click and then open.

Martin stood In the doorway, looking at Andy holding the water bottle.

"Andy?" Martin said. "We thought you left an hour ago?!"

"No," Andy said and pointed to all the coffins, "Finished those."

"I was just about to leave," Martin laughed. "Lucky I heard you otherwise you would have been here all night!"

Gerald popped his head in and then walked in, looking at Andy and then Martin.

"Thought you went home, Andy!" He said.

"I said the same," Martin said. "Nearly left the poor sod here all night!"

"Why didn't you answer when I called out earlier?" Gerald said, looking upset and concerned.

"When?" Andy asked. "Don't remember anyone coming in."

"About an hour ago," Gerald said. "I came in when it was chucking down to offer you a lift."

"I didn't hear you," Andy said. "I must have been upstairs," He said. "Or changing my batteries, they went earlier.

"I didn't see you in here," Gerald said. "So I asked the office, and no one had seen you, so we gathered you went home!"

"No," Andy shook his head. "Would have told someone if I did."

"Did you not check in the workshop?" Martin asked.

"Briefly," Gerald said. "And I called out."

"Andy is deaf you plonker," Andy laughed. "You should have checked upstairs!"

"Sorry, Andy!" Gerald said putting his hand on Andy's shoulder. "I didn't mean to do it."

"You just wanted me to do all your work," Andy laughed. "So, you locked me in here for good measure!"

"He isn't wrong," Martin smiled. "You okay Andy?"

"I am good," Andy said. "Just need the loo."

"Guess you were about to piss in a bottle?" Martin said trying not to laugh."

"Yes," Andy said. "Anyway before I run to the loo, I have done the additional coffins, and also tidied upstairs," Andy said. "Should be easier getting to the stock now."

"How did you move those?" Martin asked curiously.

"Awkwardly," Andy said. "But found a little trolley up there that proved useful."

"Silver frame with blue plastic handles?" Gerald asked.

"That's it," Andy said.

"Been looking everywhere for that!" Gerald scoffed. "It's mine by the way, Nick lost it apparently," He said. "But looks like that mystery is complete."

"Do you want a lift back?" Martin asked.

"Not if you are driving!" Andy laughed.

"Cheeky shit," Martin said. "No, Gerald is driving."

"That would be nice," Andy said. "Could you drop me at the Marina?"

"Sure," Gerald said. "How come?"

"Meeting a friend," Andy said. "And will walk the rest of the way."

"Nice," Martin said looking at his watch. "I want to lock up, so go to the toilet before you wet yourself," He looked at Gerald. "Could you bring the Hearse into the courtyard?"

"Sure," Gerald said. "How come?"

"I am getting in early to clean it," Martin said. "You are joining us for a funeral tomorrow," He said. "You have a jacket?"

"No," Andy shook his head.

"No worries," Gerald said. "We have a spare."

"Gangster funeral tomorrow," Martin said. "And I am not joking."

"You being serious?" Andy said looking at Gerald who nodded.

"Well sort of," Gerald said. "More king of the local gypsy site." Martin sighed heavily.

"Scared the shit out of you didn't he?" Gerald laughed.

"Why?" Andy asked curiously.

"You will see tomorrow," Martin said. "Might want a bulletproof vest."

"Oh give it a rest you wuss!" Gerald snapped. "Bloody big girl's blouse you are!"

# THURSDAY

Andy stepped through the double doors, looking around the room with a grin on his face. The floors are dark brown tiles, old, worn and cracked. The walls were plain bricked and sealed with laminate. The plain concrete ceiling with exposed pipework and cables, various single tube fluorescent lights, bright and harsh with one in the corner flickering. On one side of the room are various stainless still cabinets, all with posters stuck to the door, in the middle of the cabinets is a door leading to changing rooms and the rest of the building. On the other side of the room are large stainless-steel sinks and washbasins, racks with gloves, masks, and aprons. At the centre of the room are two large steel tables, complete with drainage systems. Large direct theatre lights at the centre, lighting up the tables. Next to each table is a computer station and a set of electronic sales. At the far end are double doors leading to the morgue cold storage.

"This is cool," Andy said. "I need to come back with a video camera!"

Gerald let the door close, looking at Andy curiously

"What for?" Gerald asked. "Talking to yourself?"

"To make a creepy movie," Andy said. "I have the story in my head already!"

The door opened and Martin walked in, looking at Andy and then Gerald.

"What are you two talking about?" Martin asked.

"Andy wants to make a film here," Gerald said.

"Oh wow that would be cool," Martin nodded in appreciation. "Do you need an actor?" He pointed to himself.

"I guess you would be suitable considering it's a horror," Gerald scoffed, laughing softly.

"You are pushing your luck," Martin grinned. "Do you do acting then Andy?" Martin asked curiously.

"Yes," Andy nodded.

"You any good?" Martin said.

"Well, you think I like you don't you?" Andy said, keeping a straight face as Gerald started giggling.

"Oh, charming!" Martin exclaimed. "And to think I liked you!" The double doors were burst open with a patient trolley and the woman looked up at Martin, Gerald, and Andy.

"What are you three after?" She asked.

The woman is tall and slim with long curly blonde hair and clear-rimmed glasses, wearing dark grey scrubs and white theatre shoes.

"This is Debbie," Martin said. "She prefers Debs though."

"Only the nice people get to call me Debs," She said walking over. "You on a collection?"

"No," Martin said. "This is Andy."

"Oh yes!" She said. "I forgot!"

"Brain like a sieve this one," Martin said.

"Arse," Debs poked her tongue out, holding out her hand to shake Andy's' "Nice to meet you, Andy," She said looking at Martin.

"You can call me Debs."

"Typical," Martin scoffed.

"Are you okay to have Andy with you for an hour or two?" Gerald asked. "If it's not a problem."

"Not a problem at all," Debs smiled. "Marcia already contacted me."

"Oh did she now?" Martin moaned. "So you let me explain everything this morning even though you had already been asked?"

"Yes," Debs nodded, a smile on her face. "You barely listen anyhow!"

"Bloody cheek," Martin said. "Anyway, Andy," He tapped Andy on the shoulder. "Debs here is an embalmer slash make-up artist."

"Oh right," Andy said.

"You up for watching me doing some make-up?" She asked Andy. "Not squeamish are you?"

"He is as dark as you are," Gerald said. "Lives in a world of horror this lad!"

The door opened and Sonja walked in, groaning when she saw Gerald and Martin.

"What the hell are you two doing here?" She asked. "Hi, Andy!" She smiled. "Are they looking after you?"

"Leaving him with me for an hour, " Debs said. "They probably want to hit the pub."

"You will have more fun with Debs," Sonja said. "Imagine," She paused. "A day with two boring old men, or a day with our sexy little specialist?"

Andy is lost for words.

"Aww," Sonja said. "Shy are you?"

Andy shook his head trying to hide it, but it was obvious he was.

"How come you are here?" Gerald said. "Didn't think they let you out of your doom room."

"Helping out," Sonja said. "Patrick is off sick."

"How come?" Martin asked.

"Food poisoning," Sonja said. "Turns out the chicken he had the other night wasn't cooked properly."

"Oh no you are kidding," Debs said. "The poor sod!"

"He was on a date as well," Sonja chuckled. "He took her home, got comfortable and when she removed her top, he ran to the toilet, violently sick."

"That is hysterical!" Martin burst out laughing.

"Don't be mean!" Debs said.

"She ended up walking out, offended," Sonja took a deep breath, trying not to laugh. "Took her a day to come round when she realised."

"Poor bastard," Gerald said. "Doesn't have much luck does he?"

"No," Sonja said. "I have three bodies to sort out this morning," Sonja looked at her watch. "I'll embalm and Debs is doing the make-up."

"Hope you have a strong stomach mate," Gerald said.

"Ah the bodies won't bother me," Andy said confidently.

"I wasn't talking about the bodies," Gerald moved closer to the door. "I am talking about these two!"

"Get lost!" Sonja said shoving him out of the door. "We will show Andy what we have planned today and then you can pick him up in an hour."

"Any autopsies today?" Andy asked curiously.

"Afraid not," Sonja said. "But when I do, I'll see if I can get you to watch."

"Sick," Gerald said. "Kids nowadays, come on you!" He pulled at Martin's shirt. "We need to get back."

"Anything exciting?" Debs asked.

"Sorting out insurance for me to drive the vehicles," Martin said.

"Oh yes," Sonja said. "You got your arse suspended didn't you?!"

"No need to share it with the world," Martin huffed.

"Shouldn't have been driving like a teenager in a hearse!" She scoffed. "Serves you bloody right, now get out of my morgue." Martin muttered and followed Gerald through the doors, giving Andy a thumbs up as he left.

"Right Andy," Debs said. "What we will do is show you the three bodies we are dealing with and you can watch," She said. "You will have to stand behind a screen, don't want any random fluids ending up where they shouldn't"

A bell sounded and Sonja looked at the door, waiting.

"Any time now," Sonja said impatiently.

A trolley bashed through the door, slamming it open and both Debs and Sonja flinched, the loud noise caused Andy to jump in fright.

The trolley was pushed through by a tall overweight man in black trousers and a white shirt, he was bald with a thin goatee. A body is on the trolley, covered in a white sheet, a black jacket and blankets draped over the centre.

"Jesus Christ Brian!" Debs snapped. "What have I said about using the trollies to open doors?"

"Sorry," Brian said. "Habit."

"It's disrespectful to the bodies," Sonja said. "As well as the doors."

"Cannot open them," Brian said. "Got problems with my wrists from constantly opening doors."

Sonja rolled her eyes.

"How are you love?" Brian said. "Long time no see."

"Let's not forget she moved to get away from you!" Debs laughed.

"You!" Brian said noticing Andy. "What are you doing here?"

"Someone is rude," Sonja said. "Andy is doing work experience with the undertakers," She looked at Andy. "Do you know Andy?"

"I do," Brian said. "He let me down last week."

"How?" Sonja said.

"I was doing work experience with the porters," Andy said. "I was sent to the wrong place which resulted in being late, but he wouldn't have it."

"I didn't know that," Brian said. "The school updated me."

"And I was basically the odd job boy," Andy said. "Making tea and coffee, washing up, cleaning the toilets."

"Cleaning toilets!" Sonja said. "Since when do porters do any of that?"

"He was being punished," Brian said. "For being late on his first day."

"I think it was more like, what can we give the deaf person to do," Andy chuckled. "Like the Victorian times all over again."

"It wasn't that bad," Brian said.

"I made twenty cups of tea and coffee, and washed up all the cups," Andy said. "And then you wanted me to clean the toilets!" He groaned. "You have someone there that clearly cannot shit straight!"

Debs burst out laughing, her hand going to her mouth as she quietened.

"I wasn't made very welcome or shown anything," Andy said. "So I left."

"Got to start somewhere," Brian said.

"Come on Brian," Sonja said. "How are you supposed to sell a job if you take the piss?"

"Jeff was going to spend the day with him," Brian said.

"Jeff?!" Sonja scoffed. "That pervert!"

"Oh come on!" Brian said. "He never knew her real age!"

"I rest my case!" Sonja scoffed.

"Anyway," Debs said. "Can we get this booked before it either walks or rots?"

"Right," Brian said. "We have here a Brian Stokes."

Andy laughed.

"Alright, alright, get it over with," Brian said. "Passed away in geriatrics."

"Cause?" Sonja asked.

"Old age they said," Brian said. "He was found at home last week, confused, dehydrated, malnourished and hypothermic."

"Hypothermic in this heat?!" Debs exclaimed.

"Tell me about it!" Brian huffed.

"What's with the coat and blankets," Sonja said. "Not appropriate."

"There is a reason for that," Brian said. "We have no casket trollies, so we had to bring him down on here, but there was a little problem."

"What?" Sonja asked.

Brain moved the jacket and blankets.

Debs yelped and started laughing, along with Sonja.

The sheet was raised, revealing the body had an erection, turning the sheet into a little tent.

"Bet you have never seen anything like that before?" Brian coughed, trying not to look.

"Actually I have," Sonja said looking at Debs who is still laughing, nodding in agreement.

"He died happy," Andy said. "Wonder what he was up to before he died!"

"I don't want to know," Brian said. "I wheeled him out and didn't even notice until the matron told me to go back inside!" Brian moaned. "There was me about to push a body with an erection through the ward in prime visiting times.

Debs laughed louder, turning away, and trying to calm herself down.

"She ain't normal," Brian said. "Most girls her age are out getting married and making babies!"

"I prefer to make money," Debs said. "Not into all that baby-making rubbish."

"You a dyke?" Brian asked bluntly.

"Dyke?" Andy said. "What is that?"

"You not heard of that?" Brian said. "Girls that like muff."

"Right that is enough," Sonja said. "Not having that kind of talk around here, so where is the paperwork?"

"On its way," Brian said. "Want me to put it away?"

"No," Sonja said. "You can bugger off."

Brian shrugged his shoulders.

"If you want a fresh start," Brian said. "Come and join us again and I will give you a proper show around."

"Thanks," Andy said. "But I would rather eat glass."

"Fair enough," Brian said, picking up the jacket and blankets. "Bye."

Brian left, slamming the doors as he left.

"Idiot," Sonja said. "If I hear him say that one more time, I am going to report him."

"Stuck in the past," Debs said. "What are we doing with Brian and his pole?" She giggled.

"Behave," Sonja rolled her eyes. "I will put him into cold storage, do you want to show Andy the three bodies we are working on."

"One is pretty bad," Debs said. "Might be an idea to give that a miss."

"It's okay," Andy said. "I am fine with it."

"You sure?" Debs said. "It's bad."

Debs looked at Andy in confusion, she stuttered and took a deep breath.

"Are you studying how to be dead or something?" She scoffed. "Seems an odd work experience placement."

"Wait for it," Sonja said knowingly. "It's not what you think it is."

"I struggled to find places, and the undertakers stood out," Andy said. "Plus, I love horror."

"And there it is," Sonja smiled.

"Me too!" Debs exclaimed. "Seen any horror films that scared you?"

"No," Andy said thinking. "Grew up with horror films, so they don't have any effect on me."

"For me, it was the American Werewolf in London," She groaned. "The scene with the guy in the hospital bed in the forest!" She laughed. "Made me jump every bloody time!"

"I love that film," Andy said. "I had a gathering on my tenth birthday," He chuckled. "A guy I went to school with went home crying in the first five minutes!"

"How old was he?" Sonja asked.

"Ten as well," Andy said.

"Poor sod," She rolled her eyes. "Probably a regular in the psych wards now!"

Debs laughed aloud, her hand going to her mouth.

"She likes to laugh," Sonja said. "Loudly."

"Someone has to!" Debs said. "Come on, follow me."

Andy followed Debs through the double doors and on their right the entrance to a refrigeration unit, the humming from it nearly blocking out their voices.

"That is loud!" Andy said. "Bloody hell!"

"Needs repair," Sonja said. "It works, it just sounds like a jet engine!"

"This is where we keep our lunch," Debs said. "Sandwiches, cakes and drinks," She nodded.

Andy looked at her, not quite sure what to believe and then looked at Sonja.

"She is winding you up," Sonja said.

"Behave," Andy said to Debs.

"So," Debs said and laughed. "The three bodies have been placed here," She tapped her hand on the door, the thumps echoing. "It's a walk-in refrigerator," She pointed to the door behind Andy. "That door leads to the main storage where we can store up to thirty bodies."

"What happens if you run out of room?" Andy asked curiously.

"Why, what are you planning?" She grinned. "Can I help?"

Sonja sighed heavily.

"No sense of humour that one," Debs giggled.

"It's so bloody hot!" Sonja moaned. "Can we go inside?"

"Patience!" Debs said. "Hungry or something?"

Sonja looked up, thinking, and then nodded.

"If it becomes full," Debs explained. "We ask other hospitals, failing that we can hire portable storage units, but touch wood," She touched her forehead with her index finger. "That has never happened here, as far as I know?" She looked at Sonja for clarification.

"No," Sonja said. "The only time it did was when the builders accidentally cut through the power line and blew out the electrics, so we had to get a portable unit."

"Bloody hell," Andy exclaimed. "Bet that was a mess."

"We had about ten bodies," Sonja said trying to remember. "This was ten years ago, so trying to remember, but we called some local undertakers who helped us out," She smiled. "I remember Marcia coming down with her son to collect some bodies, poor sod was hungover."

"Owch!" Andy said. "Bet that was nice!"

Debs opened the door and Andy looked in curiously.

There was barely enough room for the three trollies, two side by side and one at an angle, just so the door could be closed. All three bodies are covered with white sheets.

"Sure you want to see this?" Debs said. "I don't want the blame for traumatising you for the rest of your life?"

"I will be fine," Andy said. "I promise."

"It's okay," Sonja said. "I will catch up with him after."

"Okay," Debs said. "You sound like my kind of people," She punched him gently in the arm. "First up we have," She paused as she read the name on the notes on the trolley. "A Mr Erics who passed away from the effects of a stroke at the local swimming baths," Debs said. "He never came up after a dive, massive stroke and drowned."

"Exercise is bad for you," Andy said. "That is why I don't do it." Sonja started to laugh, shaking her head as she pulled the trolley out, slowly pulling back the sheet to reveal a man in his sixties with an autopsy scar on his chest.

"Family requested a viewing, so we will give him a touch-up and some colour," She said.

"Fair enough," Andy said. "A quick one then."

"Yes," Sonja said, covering the body and pushing it to the side.

"The next is a sad case, so it may be a shock," She pulled the trolley, looking at the notes. "This is Aiden," She said. "Suicide, they found him in Devil's Dyke, hanging from a tree."

"That is sad," Andy said. "Devils Dyke?" He asked. "What is that?"

"It's a country park next to Brighton," Sonja said. "Woods, fields and tons of hills," She groaned. "Quite nice if you like all that crap."

"Sonja hates nature," Debs said. "Happy with her concrete utopia!"

"I don't hate it!" Sonja complained. "I just don't like walking in it."

"Anyway," Debs smiled. "Back to work."

She pulled back the sheet to reveal the boy, no older than fifteen years old. Long dark hair brushed back. His neck was heavily bruised and torn from the hanging, his broken neck obvious. His autopsy scar is fresher.

"Another viewing," Debs said. "Will tidy up his neck, so it isn't so noticeable.

"Do they know why?" Andy asked.

"Why what?" Debs asked.

"Why he killed himself?" Andy said.

"Problems at school," Debs said. "And he was struggling to come out."

"Come out where?" Andy asked curiously.

"Come out as gay," Debs said. "Homosexual."

"Okay," Andy said. "Must have been hard."

"Yeah," Debs said. "I was there when the parents identified him, it was heartbreaking."

"I bet," Andy said.

Sonja pulled the trolley to the side so Debs could get to the third trolley.

"Okay Andy," Sonja said. "This one will be gory, so I just need to warn you."

"Sure," Andy said. "How gory is gory?"

"Seen the evil dead?" Debs asked.

Andy nodded.

"Worse," Debs said, trying not to laugh.

"Tell him the story first," Sonja said.

"No it's fine," Andy said. "Show me and then tell me the story." Sonja looked at Debs and nodded in agreement.

"This poor guy is the victim of a road traffic accident," Debs picked up the paperwork from the trolley. "He was on his way to work, stopped to do his shoelace up and due to having headphones, he didn't see the bus coming down the road."

"Splat!" Andy said. "Poor sod."

"The bus took the wrong turning, turns out there was oil in the road, discarded by a local fish and chip shop," Debs sighed. "Hit him and dragged him down the road."

"It was in the local," Sonja added. "The bus driver went the wrong way down a one-way system."

"A traumatic accident, killed instantly," Debs said. "He was severed midriff, an arm torn off and half of his face scrapped off," She held the sheet. "Ready?"

Andy nodded.

Debs pulled back the sheet, only to reveal the body from the chest up. The arm had been sewn back into place. The face is missing most of the cheek on the left side, showing teeth, muscle, and jawbone. One of the eyes is open, misted and glazed over, looking directly at Andy. The long brown hair is matted with blood, the scalp torn at the back.

"We were concerned about the ear being missing," She said pointing to the side of his head, leaning over. "However a recent photo revealed he lost it years ago."

"Bloody hell," Andy said looking closer. "Would he have survived?"

"Unlikely," Sonja said. "The shock most likely killed him, or the massive loss of blood."

"And guess what?" Debs said.

"What?" Andy asked.

"They want a viewing," Debs shook her head.

"No way!" Andy said. "That is going to be nuts."

"He had a young wife," Sonja said. "Twin girls."

"So they gave me a recent photograph and asked to have his face rebuilt for a viewing," Debs said. "Did our best to talk them out of it, but some people have to."

"How do you feel?" Sonja asked.

"Me?" Andy asked curiously. Sonja nodded.

"Doesn't feel real," Andy said, smiling and then chuckling. "Feels like I am on the set of a horror film."

"Just like me!" Debs laughed. "Any questions?"

"No," Andy said. "Well actually yes."

"Shoot!" Debs said, covering up the body and crossing her arms.

"Who?" Andy asked.

"Who what?" Debs said, unsure what he meant.

"You said shoot, I asked who!" Andy laughed. "Kidding, what is the worst thing you have ever seen?"

"Body wise?" Debs asked.

Andy nodded.

"I know the answer to this one," Sonja said.

"That is a difficult question," Debs said, the smile disappearing from her face.

"You don't have to say," Andy said. "I am sorry."

"It's okay," Debs said. "It was on my first week and I was working with Sonja."

"We had a young girl," Sonja said. "House fire."

"Oh no," Andy said.

"She was burnt from toe to her neck," Debs said. "She fought it, but the burns were too extensive."

Debs breathed in deeply.

"They wanted a viewing, even though it was advised against," Sonja explained. "So Debs managed to cover up the burns on the girl's neck and under her chin, and she was dressed in her favourite outfit."

"We hid her hands under a teddy bear, stitched it to her clothes so they couldn't see them," She breathed out. "It went well and the parents thanked me, hugged me and made me ugly cry with them."

"That is really sad," Andy said.

"Can I ask you a question?" Debs asked.

"Sure," Andy nodded.

"Have you ever been to a viewing?" She asked.

Andy shook his head.

"No," He said. "I was asked if I wanted to see my uncle, but I said no," Andy paused. "It didn't feel right, to be honest, and I watched him change over the months."

"What did he die of?" Sonja asked.

"Cancer," Andy said. "Aggressive and fast."

"Sorry to hear that," Debs said. "Was that recently?"

"Last year," Andy nodded.

"Does this not bother you?" Debs said. "At all?"

"No," Andy said. "It is all good."

Gerald opened the door, looking at Andy and then the bodies.

"That was quick," Sonja said looking at her watch.

"Change of plan," Gerald said. "Arthur is off sick, so how do you feel about helping with pallbearing?"

"Paul what?" Andy said curiously and confused.

"Pallbearing," Debs giggled. "Carrying a coffin."

"Oh!" Andy realised. "Sure," He nodded.

"Aww!" Debs said. "Thought you liked us!"

Andy looked at Gerald and then at Debs.

"I do," Andy said. "But he needs help more than you do!" He whispered.

"I bloody heard that!" Gerald said. "Come on, there is a lunch in it!"

"Sold," Andy said. "It was good to meet you."

"You too," Debs said, reaching forward, grabbing hold of Andy, and hugging him. "If I don't see you, I hope all the dreams work out for you."

"Thanks," Andy said, awkwardly hugging back. "Maybe meet you again one day, could always binge some horror films!"

"Aww sweet," Sonja gagged in jest. "Come on, get lost!" She pulled Andy away, shoving him in Geralds Direction.

The hearse pulled up outside the church, slowly coming to a stop as the gravel crunched. Andy sat behind the passenger seat, wearing a black suit, white shirt, and a black tie. Gerald sat in the driver's seat and Martin in the passenger seat, both also wearing black suits. Martin wore a red waistcoat and a black top hat.

A coffin is loaded in the back, with flowers and wreaths surrounding it. On top of the coffin is a large wreath spelling out FATHER in roses.

"You okay?" Gerald turned around slowly.

"Warm!" Andy said breathing heavily. "And I think I have inhaled a ton of pollen and possibly a wasp."

Gerald chuckled softly.

Martin turned around, looking around.

"Remember what we discussed?" Martin said. "It's a traveller's funeral, so you may get a few odd people."

"Just a few," Gerald said. " But it will be okay."

"If you could stay with the hearse," Martin said. "While myself, Gerald, Marcia and Leanne do the flowers," He said. "Is that okay?"

"Sure," Andy said. "Happy to do anything."

"Good lad," Gerald said. "When Marcia gets out, we will follow."

Andy nodded, trying to stifle a sneeze.

"You allergic?" Martin asked.

"No," Andy said. "These flowers are strong."

"I agree with him there," Andy said. "They are a tad overwhelming."

"What will I need to do?" Andy asked. "When we take the coffin in?"

"Don't worry I will look after you," Gerald said. "You won't need to help with the pallbearing, two or three of the family want to do it, so it will be just me and possibly Leanne."

"I will lead," Martin said. "And I would like you to follow."

"Okay," Andy said.

"You are just keeping an eye on things for us," Gerald said. "Once we have laid the coffin on the altar, we step back and bow at the same time, so just follow."

"Will do," Andy nodded. "Unless heatstroke gets me."

Marcia walked up the side of the hearse and stopped, bowing for a few seconds before walking to the driver's side and knocking.

"Hello," Gerald said winding the window down fully. "Ready to go?"

"Not yet," Marcia said looking through the window. "Hello Andy," She smiled. "Thanks for coming."

Andy smiled and nodded.

"I have had a request," Marcia said. "For you."

"Me?" Andy asked. "What?"

"The old boy had a cat that died a couple of days later," Marcia said. "They want it buried with the old man."

"A cat?" Gerald said. "I gather it's hygienic and everything?"

"They have it in a coffin," Marcia said. "It is an amazing piece of work I must say."

"Fair enough," Martin said. "Are you okay to do that?"

"What do I need to do?" Andy asked.

"Carry the coffin and follow behind," Marcia said. "They want the cat's coffin placed at the head of the coffin."

"Sure," Andy nodded. "I can do that."

"Thank you," Marcia said. "The son wants to talk to you before, but don't worry, he is much nicer than he looks."

Marcia walked back to the limo parked behind the hearse.

"Why is she telling me not to worry?" Andy asked.

"No idea," Gerald said.

Andy watched in the mirror as the family started to get out of the limo, all the men wearing black suits, some in caps and some in black fedora hats.

"Blimey," Andy said softly. "It's a gangster family."

"Time to get out," Martin said.

Andy stood by the edge of the hearse, greeting the mourners as they took it in turns to pay their respects. The flowers and wreaths had all been taken out, apart from the main one on top of the coffin.

A man stumbled from inside the church, looking at Andy and then slowly made his way over to him.

Wearing a black suit, white shirt, and a black tie, tight on his heavy build. He has a dark grey cap, lopsided.

"Who are you?" He asked. "You family?"

"No," Andy said.

"What are you doing here then?" The man snapped, not giving Andy a chance to respond. "I suggest you get lost before you get hurt."

"I am with the undertakers," Andy said.

"Oh," The man nodded. "Will let you off then."

Andy smiled and nodded.

"Could you grab me a whiskey in a bit?" The man said, patting Andy on the shoulder. "It's warm."

He walked away, giving Andy a thumbs up as he hurried back into the church.

"You Andy?" A tall heavily built man approached Andy, holding a decorated wooden box under one arm.

Wearing a black suit, silver waistcoat, and a black fedora with a white feather on the side, he is clean-shaven with jet-black hair.

"Yes," Andy said. "How can I help you?"

"What did he want?" The man said, indicating towards the man who had just spoken to Andy.

"Questioned if I was family and then asked me to get him a whiskey," Andy smiled.

"He is a drunk," The man scoffed. "Take no notice, if he gives you any crap you tell me."

"Will do," Andy said.

"Marcia said you will be carrying my dad's dead cat," The man said, handing Andy the box.

"Of course," Andy said, gently taking it.

"Poor little guy died a couple of days after," The man said. "Broken heart most likely."

"Sorry to hear that," Andy said, noticing the tattoos on the man's hand—one of a black widow on his right hand, and a red rose on the other.

"Appreciate it," The man said. "I will sort you out after, don't you worry about that."

"It is not a problem," Andy said.

"You deaf?" The man said noticing the hearing aids.

"Yes," Andy said. "Both ears."

"You don't seem the type," The man laughed. "You hide it well." Andy nodded.

"Anyway, better get ready," The man says, leaning forward and kissing the old man's coffin. "See you soon Dad!" He then walked back to the limo where the mourners had gathered, a dozen or so. Martin and Gerald made their way towards Andy, with Marcia and Leanne following.

"Is that the cat?" Martin asked.

"Yes," Andy said. "Doesn't smell too good."

"Thought that was you," Martin whispered.

"Funny," Andy said.

"They left it in the shed for the last few days," Marcia said. "In a fridge, but it broke down."

"Lovely," Andy said wrinkling his nose. "Not many people here," He looked around.

"This is only the immediate family," Marcia said. "There are over a hundred inside."

"There is a guy in there that wanted me to sort him out a whiskey," Andy said. "Looked and smelt like he was drunk!"

"Bit early!" Leanne said. "Jeez!"

"Just so we are aware, I, Leanne, Gerald and Martin will be pallbearing," Marcia said. "There has been a change of plans."

"How come?" Martin asked. "I thought they wanted to be pallbearers?"

"Apparently not," Marcia said. "The daughter has asked us to take over."

"Fair enough," Martin said. "Not an issue."

"Are we all ready?" Marcia asked.

"Are you seeing this?" Andy said quietly. "Two guys heading towards us with shotguns?"

Everyone suddenly turned around, watching as the two older men came towards them, holding shotguns over their shoulders. Both are in black suits, black overcoats, and black fedoras.

"You okay lads?" Marcia said sternly.

"They are not loaded," One of the men said. "Just for show."

"A warning would have been nice," Marcia said. "You scared the crap out of my team."

"Sorry about that," The other man said. "Probably should have mentioned it at the beginning."

Leanne sighed in relief.

"We will be leading the coffin," The first man said. "Is this the young lad carrying Cat?"

"Yes," Andy replied. "Did it have a name?"

"Cat," The man said.

"Yes the cat," Andy replied. "Did it have a name?"

"Cat," The second man said. "He deaf or something?" He asked Marcia.

"Yes he is," Marcia smiled and nodded.

"Sorry," The man said. "Didn't mean no offence."

"It's fine," Andy said. "So the cat is called, Cat?"

The man nodded, a grin breaking on his face.

"That is original!" Marcia said.

"The old man hated cats," The man said. "He couldn't have a dog due to his disability, so we got him a cat to keep him company, the lazy bastard never gave him and name and called him 'Cat' and that is what he got used to."

"Fair enough," Marcia said. "Are we ready to start?"

The man nodded.

"Everyone ready? Marcia looked around at the team who nodded in agreement.

Andy followed the coffin, taking short steps and focusing ahead. There are over a hundred mourners, all in black and standing in the pews, looking at the coffin as it moved slowly past them. The priest, stood behind the altar, a large wooden cross behind him and a stained-glass window behind that. Bagpipe music is playing, from the front and Andy could just about see someone playing.

Maria and Leanne are at the back, with Martin and Gerald leading, they stop at the front of the altar and slowly lower the coffin down, placing it on the edge to allow room for the cat. They all took a step back and bowed, before walking towards Andy. Gerald nods at him, indicating for him to go.

"This stinks!" Andy said in his head.

Walking around the side, Andy placed the coffin at the head of the coffin, stepped back and bowed.

Everyone started to clap and cheer, Andy looked up, confused he had done something wrong. He looked to Gerald who indicated for him to leave.

Andy then made his way to the entrance, smiling at Leanne who held the door open for him and then slowly closed it.

"Jesus!" Andy huffed as he got outside, breathing deeply.

"What's wrong?" Martin said in worry. "Are you okay?"

"The smell was bad," Andy said. "Like rotten chicken with a hint of poo!"

"Oh dear," Leanne said putting her arms across his shoulder and hugging him. "Thought you were nervous."

"No," Andy said. "Not nervous at all."

"I could smell it a little," Martin said. "Was it worse than the house?" He asked. "With the old girl?"

"Worse," Andy said. "Chicken has to be the worst I have smelt!"

"I agree," Leanne said. "Liquidated chicken," She gagged.

"Reminds me of being at my nan's last year," Andy said. "Was helping her with dinner and seems a pack of chicken she got was off," He shivered. "As soon as I opened it, it splashed in my face."

"Oh no!" Leanne groaned. "Bet that sucked."

"Let's go and stand in the shade," Marcia said. "I am about to melt!"

Andy walked over to the hearse, opened the door, and removed a bottle of water.

"You okay?" Gerald asked.

"All good thanks," Andy replied, offering water to Gerald who shook his head.

"No thanks," Gerald smiled. "You did very well today, you have picked this up well."

"I am enjoying it," Andy said. "I had fun today with Sonja and Debs."

"Dead bodies," Gerald scoffed. "Is that why?"

"Maybe," Andy chuckled.

The doors opened and a man walked out, Andy looked up and groaned.

"What's up?" Gerald said looking around at the man.

"He was off with me earlier," Andy said. "Thought I was crashing the funeral and threatened to hurt me."

"You are kidding," Gerald said. "Cheeky bastard!"

The man walked over, waving gently at Andy.

"You sorted that whiskey out yet?" He asked.

Gerald looked at Andy in confusion.

"Sorry?" Andy replied.

"Whiskey?" The man said. "Where is it?"

"We don't have alcohol," Gerald said. "You would need a bar for that."

"Where is it then?" The man demanded.

"The nearest bar is about five minutes away," Gerald said. "Right at the gates and keep walking, then you will see the Shipman's Son Pub.

"Cannot go in there," The man said. "Banned."

"We do not carry alcohol," Gerald said firmly.

"What do you carry?" The man asked.

Andy and Gerald looked at each other, and then at the man.

"Have a wild guess," Gerald said, indicating towards the hearse.

"Fair enough," The man says and walks away, stumbling and swaying towards the graveyard.

Andy sat in the front seat of the hearse, yawning loudly.

"Tired?" Gerald asked.

"Yeah," Andy said. "Was woken up late last night, never got back to sleep."

"How come?" Gerald asked curiously.

"Someone set the fire alarms off at two in the morning," Andy said. "So the whole school was out on the tennis court."

"Bloody hell," Gerald exclaimed. "How many students are there?"

"About a hundred and twenty or so," Andy said.

"Why didn't you get back to sleep?" Gerald said. "Thinking about us too much?"

"I dream a lot," Andy said. "And have an overactive imagination, so I lay there thinking too much."

"Fair enough," Gerald said. "Plus it was quite warm last night wasn't it?"

Andy nodded, drinking from the water bottle.

"I like the heat," Gerald said. "But have had enough of it now, I would love some snow right now!"

Someone knocked loudly on the window, causing Gerald to yelp in fright. It was the old boy's son that Andy had spoken to earlier. He had removed his jacket and rolled up his sleeves revealing various tattoos, spiders and an English flag on his right forearm and a swastika, crossbones, and blades on his left arm.

"Hey kid," The man said handing an envelope to Andy, "That is to say thanks, I heard you are not getting paid."

"I am on work experience," Andy said taking the envelope. "What is this?"

"A thank you," The man said giving Andy a thumbs up. "Hope to see you at the wake for a few pints," The man said, drumming his hands on top of the hearse before walking away.

"We are not going to the wake," Gerald said. "Did you see those tattoos?"

"Oh yes," Andy said. "I saw the swastika!"

"Shocking in our day and age someone would do that to themselves," Gerald shook his head.

159

"Still stuck in the past," Andy said.

"What did he give you?" Gerald asked curiously.

Andy opened the envelope to reveal one hundred in cash.

"Blimey," Andy said.

"Nice one," Gerald said. "Gotta say that was good of him."

"I'll share it with everyone," Andy said.

"Why?" Gerald scoffed. "He gave that to you, and trust me, no one will want any of it, it is yours."

Marcia hurried up to the driver's side and leaned down, sighing in relief.

"That breeze is nice," She said. "Andy, would you like to join us later for dinner?" She asked. "We are going to a local pizza restaurant."

"That would be nice," Andy said. "On one condition."

"What?" Marcia asked.

"You put this towards it," Andy said handing the envelope to her.

"What is this?" Marcia said curiously.

"The son gave Andy a hundred pounds," Gerald said. "As a thank you."

"No," Marcia said. "Keep that, he also gave me some money to treat everyone to food."

"Good of him," Gerald said.

"Could you do a collection first?" Marcia said. "I am sure you could both manage that?"

"Sure," Gerald said. "We will drop this back and grab the van, you okay with that Andy?"

"Yes," Andy said. "I need more water!"

"You and me both!" Gerald laughed. "Martin coming with us?"

"No," Marcia said. "He is coming with me, Leanne is taking the other car."

"See you later," Gerald said. "Let's go grab a van, and possibly a chocolate ice," Gerald grinned.

The van reversed onto the drive of the house, slowly backing in as close to the double doors as he could.

"Want to come with me?" Gerald said, not realising he had chocolate on his lip."

"Sure," Andy said. "Might want to clean the chocolate off your mouth, don't want you embarrassing me."

Gerald laughed, wiping his mouth with a tissue, and looking in the mirror.

"Cheeky sod!" He scoffed. "Let's go, I will let you do the talking then, got the sheet?"

Andy nodded, holding up the sheet.

"Okay, know what to do?" Gerald asked.

"Yes," Andy said. "I will be fine."

"We come here a lot," Gerald said. "One of the biggest care homes in the area."

"Constant custom!" Andy Said.

Gerald laughed, getting out of the van, Andy finished the water he had, put the bottle in the side of the door, and climbed out.

"I just need to speak to someone first," Gerald said. "So if you could go to the nurse's station and speak to the matron in charge, she will let you know the room details and hand you the relevant paperwork."

"Will be okay," Andy said. "Did the same thing with Arthur last week."

"Did Marcia tell you about Arthur?" Gerald asked curiously as they approached the double doors.

"No," Andy said. "Other than he is sick."

"Appendicitis," Gerald said. "He thought he had a stitch, only it got worse by the evening and he doubled over, cracking his head on the table."

"Shit!" And gasped.

"Don't panic," Gerald said. "The table is fine."

"Glad to hear it," Andy chuckled. "Seriously, is he okay?"

"He is fine," Gerald said. "He had surgery last night and is recovering, if we get time tomorrow we can pop in and say hello and make him laugh."

"No don't do that," Andy said shaking his head. "When I had mine out, my mother knew laughing hurt, so she bought me a joke book and kept telling me jokes."

"You are kidding!" Gerald said.

"Afraid not," Andy said. "Not sure she loves me to be honest."

"You think?" Gerald said, ringing the doorbell.

"Well she complained about the cost of a bus whenever she visited," Andy said. "Even the day I came home, they said a bus wasn't suitable so my mother reluctantly called my aunt, and then guilt-tripped me for days after my aunt damaged her wheel hitting a kerb."

"No way!" Gerald said. "How long were you in for?"

"A week," Andy said. "I had a lovely reaction to penicillin, it was a rough couple of days."

"That sucks," Gerald said, standing back when the door opened. "Hey Judy," Gerald smiled.

Judy is one of the main nurses, short and heavily built with short curly blonde hair and thick red glasses, she has an apron on and gloves, sweating heavily.

"Gerald!" She said loudly. "Thought you forgot all about me!"

"Well I usually come for the dead," Gerald smiled. "You seem very much alive."

"Who is this?" She asked, looking Andy up and down.

"Andy," Gerald said. "On work experience with us for a week."

"Morbid sod," She said. "What are you in for."

"Who are we in for?" Gerald chuckled. "Is the question."

"Oh," She said. "We lost two people in the last twenty-four hours."

"Sorry to hear that," Gerald said.

Judy sighed heavily, shaking her head slowly.

"And we have an outbreak of some kind," Judy added. "It's never-ending in this place."

"Are we safe to come in?" Gerald asked.

"Yes," She nodded. "Just avoid the rooms with the signs on the door, no dead people in those," She paused. "Well, I fucking hope not!" She laughed.

"I am just going to say hi to an old friend," Gerald said to Andy. "Pop to the nurse's station and ask for the matron," He looked at Judy. "Is it still Kathy?"

Judy nodded, screwing up her face in disgust.

"Straight down the end," Gerald pointed to a reception desk at the end of the corridor.

Andy stood at the empty reception desk, looking up and down the corridors on his left and right. Various trolleys, laundry bins and medical equipment against the wall. The reception, covered in various papers, magazines and books is a mess, a computer at the centre, plants, coffee cups and telephones. One of the telephones was ringing loudly.

"You okay there?" A male nurse came up behind Andy. "Are you a visitor?" The tall and slim Jamaican nurse asked, wearing a light blue tunic over navy blue trousers.

"I am looking for the Matron," Andy said. "Kathy I believe."

"She is with a patient," The man said. "You are?"

"Andy," Andy said. "I am with the undertaker service," Andy showed him the form.

"You look young," The man said looking Andy up and down. "How do I know you aren't a body snatcher!?" He laughed. "Junior Frankenstein by any chance?"

"Hardly going to come to a care home am I?" Andy scoffed. "Imagine the monster, limping from old joints and arthritis, with a hint of Alzheimer's and Parkinson's."

The man burst out laughing.

"I go to nightclubs for the bodies," Andy smiled.

"You old enough for nightclubs?" The man looked at Andy curiously.

"Not sharing any secrets," Andy nodded knowingly.

"Let me go and find Kathy," He walked off chuckling to himself. Several minutes passed and Kathy, tall and thin with short black hair and glasses, stepped behind the counter. She is wearing a bright red tunic and has a white hand towel over her shoulder.

"Can I help you?" She said.

Andy didn't respond, the noise of the department overwhelming him. Call buzzers alarming, patients and staff talking and a lady yelling from one of her rooms.

"Do you need help?" Kathy said.

"Hi," Andy said. "I need you to face me."

"Why?" Kathy said turning around. "What is the problem?" She said in annoyance.

"I am deaf," Andy said pointing to his ears. "I need to lipread."

"That makes sense," Kathy laughed awkwardly. "I apologise. How can I help?"

"I am with the undertaker service," Andy said. "Collection requested," He handed the form to Kathy.

"Oh yes," She said. "That is for Maryanne Smith," She looked at the form. "The family are with her at the moment, so are you okay to wait?" She handed the form back to him. "Shouldn't be long."

"That is fine," Andy said.

"Will you manage on your own?" She asked.

"Gerald is with me," Andy said. "He is visiting someone."

"Bless him," She said. "Gerald has a relative here, did he tell you?"

"No," Andy said.

"Oh shit," She said. "Don't let on I told you."

Kathy turned around, searching through the folders.

An elderly man came up behind Andy, tall, thin, and completely naked. His long grey hair is messy, his glasses resting on the edge of his nose.

Andy glanced around and suddenly looked away, trying not to laugh.

"Nurse Kathy!" He shouted. "I need the toilet!"

"Hello, Peter!" Kathy responded without turning around. "We have discussed this, you don't have to tell the staff when you want to, you can go."

"I can go?" He said, slightly confused. "Right now?"

"Yes," Kathy said turning around and exclaiming. "Peter!" She scoffed. "Why are you not wearing your clothes?"

"Having a shower!" Peter complained.

"What have we said about leaving your room with no clothes on?" She chuckled. "Go and get your dressing gown," She looked at Andy. "Sorry about that Andy."

"It's fine," Andy said biting his lip.

"So can I go to the toilet?" He asked Andy.

"I said yes Peter," Kathy said. "Go and get dressed, nobody wants to see your old bits on display!"

"Okay!" Peter said and without warning, he squatted and started to urinate.

Andy moved away as the puddle of orange liquid started to move towards him.

"Peter!" Kathy yelped. "What are you doing?!"

Peter then grunted, and it was followed by a splatter of diarrhoea which hit the floor and the wall behind him, a violent eruption followed by a stench that rolled out like an invisible wave.

"Lovely," Andy groaned and stepped back, his hand going to his nose.

"Mack!" Kathy called out. "Mack!?"

Mack, the Jamaican nurse that Andy had spoken to, came running around the corner, stopping when he saw Peter squatting in urine and excrement.

"Peter!" Mack said. "What are you doing?"

"Having a shit!" Peter said bluntly. "Kathy said I could!"

"Not in the middle of reception I didn't!" Kathy scolded him.

"I'll sort him out," Mack said. "Sorry about this," He said to Andy.

Andy shook his head, a grin on his face.

"Come on," Mach said taking hold of Peter's arm. "Let's get you in the shower."

Judy came up to the reception desk with Gerald following her, she was holding a handful of paper towels.

"What did you do Andy?" Gerald said. "I said to speak to Kathy, not crap everywhere!" Gerald groaned. "Thought you were house trained!?"

"Funny," Andy said.

"Leave him alone!" Kathy said. "Play nice!"

"Ah he is nice really," Andy said.

Judy covered the mess with the towels, shaking her head in annoyance, gagging and groaning.

"Need any help?" Kathy asked.

"I'll sort it," Judy smiled. "I am used to dealing with shit in this place."

Kathy shook her head.

"Hello Gerald," Kathy said smiling. "Good to see you, how is he?"

"Hey love," Gerald said. "He seems to be doing well," Gerald chuckled. "Pranked me as soon as I walked in."

"Pretending he couldn't remember your name?" Kathy asked.

"That's it," Gerald said.

"He did that with the doctor this morning," Kathy said. "One day it will be real and no one is going to believe him."

"I know," Gerald said. "Always a joker. What was the doctor for?"

"He was under the weather," Kathy said. "Turns out he has a little chest infection, were you not informed?"

"No," Gerald rolled his eyes. "But it's possible it's on my answer phone."

"Sorry about that," Kathy apologised.

"It's fine," Gerald smiled. "Has Andy spoken to you?"

"Yes," Kathy said. "Relatives are with her at the moment, so we need some time."

"That is okay," Gerald said. "Can we grab a drink?"

"Of course, no need to ask," Kathy said. "Help yourself to food, we had a birthday lunch and there was way too much!"

"Thank you," Gerald said. "Follow me," He poked Andy in the shoulder.

Gerald leaned against the van, with a plate of sandwiches, sausage rolls and crisps, slowly eating and looking up at the sky, his eyes closed as he soaked in the sun. Andy closed the door behind him, groaning when he stepped into the sunlight.

"Bloody vampire!" Gerald said looking around at Andy.

"It's too bloody hot!" Andy moaned. "I'd love some snow!" He bit into an apple.

"Not eating?" Gerald asked.

"Saving some space for the pizza," Andy said. "You forgotten?"

"Oh shit!" Gerald laughed. "I'll make room," He ate a few crisps. "Any updates?"

"Kathy said in five," Andy looked around. "The kids have just gone, and the granddaughter is with her."

"Good stuff," Gerald said.

"How was your visit," Andy asked.

"It's my brother," Gerald said. "I don't usually talk about it, but you seem sane enough!" Gerald chuckled, biting into a cheese sandwich. "He has Down syndrome and requires a fair bit of care."

"I understand," Andy said. "I have an uncle in care due to birth trauma."

"Oh no!" Gerald put down the sandwich, listening closer to Andy. "What happened, if you don't mind me asking."

"Forceps birth," Andy said. "Wasn't supposed to survive, he was a twin, so people think the bond helped."

"It really does," Gerald said in amazement. "How old is he?"

"Thirties or so," Andy said thinking. "I try to see him every week."

"I see my brother every day if I can," Gerald said. "He comes to mine on a Sunday for dinner, loves his Sunday roasts."

"How long has he been in care?" Andy asked.

"Not long after my mother passed," Gerald said. "Lived on his own for a while and did okay but ended up burning the house down."

"You are kidding!" Andy gasped. "Was he home?"

"No," Gerald laughed. "He put a chicken in the oven and then went to the club to pay pool, I found out when the neighbour opposite called and said there was a fire," Gerald chuckled softly, putting his plate on the bonnet of the van. "Lucky for us the neighbour next door got the hosepipe out and managed to stop it spreading, other than smoke damage, the kitchen was destroyed."

"Bloody hell," Andy said thinking. "Cannot top that, but I was at my grandparents once when my uncle was home on a day visit. My grandfather was winding him up for ages, uncle flipped out and threw a thirty-kilogram typewriter at him!" Andy exclaimed. "Missed him but left a nice dent in the wall, and the neighbour said they felt it, bearing in mind there was an alleyway!"

"Wow!" Gerald said. "That is crazy!"

The door opened and Kathy stood holding the door and leaning out.

"She is ready," Kathy said. "The family dressed her."

"How come?" Gerald asked.

"It was requested by the patient," Kathy said. "Her death was expected and the doctor saw her yesterday, all the relevant information is in the folder."

"Thanks, Kathy," Gerald said, picking up the plate and finishing the crisps. "Could you grab the trolley, Andy?" Gerald said. "Meet me at the end of the room."

"Will do," Andy said. "At this point, I am only thinking of pizza!"

"Bloody hell," Gerald said. "I am looking forward to a cold beer."

"Will you two shut up!" Kathy snapped. "I have another four hours of this crap!"

"Shut up Andy," Gerald smiled.

Gerald made his way into the building, following Kathy. Andy walked round to the van, looking at his watch and stifling a yawn.

# FRIDAY

Opening the door and stepping out of the hearse, Andy pulled the seat forward to let Leanne out. He looked up at the large church and then behind him at the farmer's fields. The first of two limos had shown up and it had started to rain slightly, the dark clouds hovering over the church.

"Wonder where the second limo is?" She said. "Hope there is nothing wrong."

Martin got out from the passenger side of the limo, straightening up his jacket as he made his way over to the hearse.

"Everything okay?" Leanne asked.

"Yes," Martin said. "You all okay?"

Leanne nodded.

"The mother had a panic attack in the car," Martin said. "She wants to make some changes to the entrance."

"What kind of changes?" Leanne asked.

"She has asked for the youngest person to carry the coffin in," Martin said.

"I am fine to do that," Leanne said. "Marcia has already asked me to."

"No," Martin said. "She saw Andy and asked if he could."

Andy looked at Martin curiously and then at Leanne.

"What?" He said. "I didn't catch that."

"How do you feel about carrying the coffin?" Leanne asked.

Andy looked at the steps and then at Leanne.

"My balance is really bad," Andy said. "But if it helps, I am happy to."

"I am fine with it," Leanne said.

"Me too," Martin added.

Gerald got out from the hearse, doing up his suit jacket.

"What have I missed," He asked.

"They want Andy to carry the coffin," Leanne said.

"Perfect," Gerald said. "He will do a great job."

"We had a worrying time on the drive here," Leanne said. "Going to have to visit the garage later."

"Why?" Martin asked, looking at the hearse.

"Red light came up on the dash," Gerald said. "And the engine made some funny noises and cut out at the traffic lights at the end of the street."

"I wondered why you started the engine," Martin said. "Thought you stalled it."

"Behave!" Gerald scoffed. "I don't stall engines."

"You okay to run it to the garage after?" Martin asked. "I will call ahead, we have a fast-track account."

"That is if it starts," Gerald smiled slightly. "It cut out as soon as I pulled up."

"Shit," Martin said. "I am popping into the church to check if all is good."

Martin walked away, hurrying up the steps, his hands on the sides of his jacket.

"So what do I have to do?" Andy asked nervously.

"I will go through it with you," Leanne said. "Don't overthink it, it's an honour really."

The door of the limo closed and a woman walked towards the hearse, stopping in front of the limo, her hand going to her mouth as she stared at the hearse.

"Hold on a minute," Leanne said, walking over to the woman. The woman is wearing red trousers, a white shirt, and a red jacket. Her long black hair is tied back, and she is holding a small teddy bear.

"Are you okay?" Leanne said. "Can I help with anything?"

"I wanted to speak to the boy," She said pointing to Andy. "But I can't, I feel sick!" She looked at the hearse."

"It's okay," She said and waved Andy over.

And quickly walked over, smiling softly.

"Hello," Andy said.

"This is the mum," Leanne said. "She wants to have a chat."

"Sure," Andy said.

Andy moved closer and the woman put her hand on Andy's arm.

"Can you carry my little girl?" She asked, her voice trembling. "Please?"

"I would be more than happy to," Andy said.

"Thank you," She cried. "Thank you so much!" She burst into tears, grabbing hold of Andy, and hugging him. Her grip on his arm tightened.

175

Andy was taken by surprise, looking at Leanne with his eyes widened.

"It's okay," Andy said.

A man got out of the limo and got hold of the woman, helping her back into her seat and gently closing the door as she was consoled by her husband.

The man is wearing a light blue suit with a white shirt, and a plastic bag under his arm. His hair is short, with red spots dyed randomly.

"Sorry about that," The man said. "It has hit her hard."

"Losing a child is never easy," Leanne said.

"Is this the kid that is carrying my niece?" He asked.

"This is Andy," Leanne smiled. "Yes."

"Can you wear this?" He said handing the bag to Andy. "It's a jacket, don't worry it is clean."

"Sure," Andy said and took it off him.

"Thanks," The man said, getting back into the limo.

Andy and Leanne made their way back to the hearse.

"What was that about?" Gerald asked.

"Just confirming the request," Leanne said. "Andy they have something for Andy to wear."

Andy opened the bag and groaned.

"You have to be kidding me," Andy said. "No way!"

"What is it?" Leanne said looking into the bag.

Andy pulled out the bright red jacket with yellow spots and on the back is a photograph of the little girl, embroidered into it.

"Oh dear," Gerald said. "That colour won't do you justice."

"It's only for a few minutes," Leanne said. "And for the parents."

"I know," Andy said and handed the jacket to Leanne. "Hold that a second."

Andy took off the black jacket, handing it to Gerald who placed it on the back seat of the hearse.

"The things I do!" He said taking the jacket from Leanne and putting it on. "A little bit too big."

"Yeah," Leanne said. "Just a bit!"

"Let's run Andy through the process," Gerald said. "We won't have long once the other car arrives."

Andy stood looking at the twenty-plus steps leading to the church, each step worn from years of use and the elements. He looked down at the small coffin white coffin, decorated with pictures of balloons and streamers in multiple bright colours. It was slightly raining, the sun breaking through the clouds glinting off the stone steps.
Several feet from him stood the parents, both dressed in red trousers and jackets, their shirts in white. Behind them two young wearing multi-coloured outfits and holding yellow balloons.

"You can go now," Gerald said.

Andy turned around, looking at Gerald, Martin and Leanne standing on the edge of the path with their backs against the hearse, the back full of various flowers and wreaths.

"Everything will be fine," Leanne said, just take it slow.

"Whatever you do," Martin said. "Don't drop it!" He chuckled softly. "Break a leg!"

177

Andy groaned softly as he turned around.

Andy slowly and carefully took each step, one at a time, looking dead ahead and occasionally glancing down to look at the steps.

"Breathe," He said to himself. "Nearly there."

As he approached the final step, his balance swayed and he felt himself falling back. He suddenly leaned forward and his foot slipped off the step, causing him to jolt forward.

"Oh shit!" He yelped and dropped the coffin, falling face down on the stones and cracking his nose.

The coffin bounced off the first step and went into a roll, thumping against every step.

Andy turned around, holding his nose as blood erupted from it and ran down his face, everything turned to slow motion.

The coffin, spun as it fell, the horrified look on the families' faces as the coffin got closer and closer.

Martin, Gerald and Leanne, their mouths open in shock.

"Fuck!" Andy screamed in his head, the rain falling harder.

The coffin hit the ground with a crunching thud, and the lid flew off and flipped into the road, followed by a doll which was launched from the coffin and landed in front of the woman, smashing as if it were made of glass.

The woman let out a scream and fainted, the man attempting to catch her and the two children running away in terror.

"Andy?" The voice boomed. "Are you daydreaming?"

Andy blinked, looking at the steps in front of him. He took a deep breath and turned around, looking at Leanne.

"What are you thinking about?" Leanne asked. "You look nervous!"

"Nothing," Andy said. "Just panicking deep inside."

"It will be fine," She said. "As Gerald explained, take each step slowly and pause when you get to the top," Leanne turned around as the father approached them, holding a pink umbrella.

"Everything okay?" He asked.

"All good," Leanne said. "Andy has agreed to carry the coffin into the church."

"I appreciate it, mate," The man said, his eyes wet and bloodshot. "We all do."

"Happy to help," Andy said.

"We will be ready once my mother arrives," The man said. "The other car is delayed."

"No problems sir," Leanne said. "We are ready."

Martin and Gerald stood at the foot of the hearse, under an umbrella.

"So run through it again with me," Leanne said. "What are you going to do?"

"Martin and Gerald will remove the coffin from the hearse," Andy explained. "I will then step forward, take the coffin from them, turn and make my way to the steps," Andy said.

"Good," She said smiling. "I will be at the top of the steps to give you indications."

Andy nodded.

"I pause at the steps," Andy took a breath. "Once you indicate that the family is ready, I then make my way to the top, slowly and gently until I get to the top, pausing again."

"I will bow," Leanne said. "Once I straighten up and the music starts, you then make your way to the altar," Leanne explained. "Take a step, count to two, take a step and so on."

Andy nodded, his heart pounding so hard in his chest he could feel the blood rushing in his ears.

"Then what?" Leanne asked.

"Once I get to the alter, I pause," Andy said. "And then place the coffin, from the front, facing the mourners."

"Brilliant," Leanne patted him on the arm. "How do you place the coffin?"

"On the side, so everyone can see the picture," Andy said. "How old was she?"

"She didn't quite make it to two years old," Leanne said softly. "Heart failure."

"Poor kid," Andy said.

"She loved her colours," Leanne said. "Hence everyone wearing colourful clothes."

"Not seen anyone in black," Andy said. "Apart from us."

Marcia walked over, with a long black overcoat down to her shoes.

"How are we doing?" She asked.

"Good," Leanne said. "Just ran through everything with Andy."

"And how are you feeling Andy?" Marcia asked. "I have faith in you."

180

"I am okay," Andy said. "just nervous."

"You will be fine," Leanne said. "Just don't overthink things."

"I am more impressed at the amount of pizza you put away last night," Marcia said. "Did you finish the rest at school?"

"I had it for breakfast," Andy said smiling.

"Pizza for breakfast?!" Marcia exclaimed.

"Like a typical bloke!" Leanne scoffed.

"Either that or someone else has it," Andy said. "I live with animals."

"The jacket suits you," Marcia smiled. "Thank you for wearing it."

"Not like I could refuse," Andy said. "It's so bright I need factor fifty!"

Marcia chuckled.

"Heads up," Leanne said quietly.

The father made his way over, nodding at Marcia.

"We are ready to start," He said.

"Thank you," Marcia said, following the man over to the several family members.

"You will be fine," Leanne said, making her way up the steps. Andy watched as she arrived at the top, standing on the side of the entrance.

Andy walked to the rear of the hearse, standing an arm's length from Martin and Gerald.

"Proud of you mate," Gerald said softly and grinning. "You are a good kid."

"Let's focus," Martin said.

Martin and Gerald pick up the coffin, moving sideways until they are in line with Andy. After a few seconds, they handed it to Andy who took the coffin from them, holding it carefully. He then walked to the edge of the steps, looking up at Leanne who nodded indication.

"Chill out," Andy said in his head. "You will be fine."

Andy then took the first step, pausing slightly and then took each step, one after another. It felt like an eternity, his heart pounding and his head screaming. The vision of his fall tormented and teased him. He arrived at the top of the step, looking into the church and then at Leanne who smiled briefly.

Andy stood at the top of the steps, waiting for the music to kick in however the sound of the rain muffled it.

Leanne looked at him and mouthed him to go.

Andy walked through the packed church, the mourners all standing, dressed in various bright-coloured clothes and hats, holding balloons, streamers and presents. He tried not to look, staring ahead at the altar with a pink blanket draped over it.

After what feels like a lifetime, he arrives at the altar and stops before bowing.

"Idiot," Andy said to himself.

He walked around the back of the Altar and placed the coffin down, slowly, and gently with the photo facing the mourners. He then stepped back and bowed for a few seconds.

Andy then joined Marcia who stood in front of the altar as she bowed and then turned, making her way to the entrance. Andy stood in front of the Altar and bowed, stepping backwards, his eyes caught the priest as he walked into view.

"What the hell?!" Andy said in his head, his eyes widened as he bit down on his tongue, trying not to laugh.

The priest was dressed up as a clown, with yellow oversized shoes, red trousers, a bright multi-coloured top and bright yellow hair. His face is white, with red circles on the cheeks and a bright green nose. Various people laughed softly as he approached the alter, with a gentle smile on his face.

"Welcome everyone," The priest said.

Everyone then threw streamers and balloons into the air, a mixture of bright colours. Some people cheered and clapped.

A balloon bounced off Andy's head, landing in front of the coffin. The priest looked at Andy, shaking his head and smiling.

"Please don't talk to me," Andy said in his head. "I am never going to lipread you!"

As the music died down, Andy turned, making his way towards the entrance, fighting against the grin that wanted to break out.

The doors closed and Andy made his way down the steps where Marcia, Martin and Gerald stood by the Hearse, Leanne followed him, her hand on his back.

"Well done mate," She said smiling. "You did great."

"Messed up though," Andy said.

"How?" Leanne asked curiously.

"I stopped and bowed at the front," Andy said. "When I should have gone behind."

"It was beautiful," Leanne said. "You handled it well so don't worry."

As they got to the bottom, Marcia started to clap and Andy flinched.

"What was that for?" Marcia asked.

"Thought I was going to get beaten for messing up," Andy chuckled nervously.

"Messing up?" Marcia said looking at Martin and Gerald who shook their heads in confusion.

"He stopped at the front and bowed," Leanne said shrugging her shoulders. "No biggie considering he saved it."

"It was good," Marcia said. "I am impressed," She looked at Martin. "Might replace you with Andy!" she laughed.

"Did anyone see what I saw," Andy asked. "Or am I dreaming?"

"What did you see?" Marcia asked.

"The priest dressed as Ronald bloody McDonald?!" Andy exclaimed.

Leanne started laughing, with the rest of them joining in.

"I must admit we wanted to see how you reacted," Marcia said. "We all knew it was going to happen."

"Oh, charming!" Andy scoffed.

"He is the brother of the father," Leanne said. "The little girl loved clowns, bright colours and all that," Leanne said. "So when they went along with the colourful funeral, they wanted it to be a happy celebration rather than doom and gloom."

"That is sweet," Andy said. "What was the music?" He asked. "I could barely hear it."

"Something they heard at a circus," Marcia said. "A group of clowns piss arsing about like my undertakers do regularly."

"Did you just swear?" Gerald asked sternly. "That is five pounds in the jar."

"How about lunch?" Marcia asked. "Will that shut you up?

"It's a start," Gerald nodded and then smiled.

"What time are you going, Andy?" Martin asked.

"One," Andy said. "Going to miss working with you."

"Aw that is sweet," Martin said.

"No not you," Andy shook his head. "I was talking to Leanne." Leanne grabbed him from behind and hugged him.

"I will remember that," Gerald scoffed.

"Will miss you too," Andy said. "You have been like the grandfather I never had!"

Gerald laughed and Martin sniggered.

"What are you sniggering about?" Gerald poked him.

"He meant great grandfather!" Martin said.

"Cheeky so and so!" Gerald scoffed. "I am getting in the vehicle," Gerald said opening the door. "I need to sit for a bit."

"Can I have a quick word, Andy?" Marcia asked.

"Sure," Andy said.

Andy followed Marcia to the first limo, standing under a tree to avoid the light rain.

"How have you found it with us?" She asked.

"I have really enjoyed it," Andy said. "The team are amazing, friendly and welcoming."

"I had a chat with Martin," She said. "As you know we are advertising shortly, and also, don't repeat this just yet, but Arthur is going to retire."

"Oh no," Andy said. "That is a shame."

"I know," Marcia said. "He has some medical issues."

"Give him my best," Andy said. "I liked him."

"I will do," Marcia said. "How would you feel about working for us?"

Andy is loss for words.

"Working for you?" Andy said. "As in a job?"

Marcia nodded.

"That is an amazing offer," Andy said. "But I am planning to do an extra year and then go to college, to do performing arts."

"I know," Marcia said. "I wanted to give the option," She sighed. "Think about it, would love to get you on board by the end of the year."

"I will think about it," Andy said.

"I know you live in Kent," She said. "And more than happy to help with organising accommodation."

"Thanks," Andy said. "I will think about it."

"Go back with Leanne and help them with the flowers," Marcia said. "Then we can all grab some food once this is finished, well one on carrying the coffin, you did well."

Andy smiled and walked away, hurrying over to Leanne as she pulled out two large wreaths and handed them to Andy.

Andy sat on the desk, still wearing the bright red jacket with yellow spots. Miss Fleet sat opposite him with a grin on her face. She is wearing a light blue summer dress with a thin white cardigan.

"Thank you for seeing me," She said. "Is there a story behind the jacket?" She asked curiously.

"I took part in a funeral for a child today," Andy said. "The mum asked me to wear it."

"Doesn't seem like funeral attire," She said.

"Everyone was dressed in colourful clothing," Andy said. "It was a circus."

"I doubt it was a circus," She scoffed.

"There was a clown," Andy added bluntly.

"A clown?" Miss Fleet exclaimed. "Why?"

"It was the priest," Andy said. "The uncle of the little girl, so they went with a," Andy groaned and stuttered. "Trying to think of the word."

"Theme?" She said.

"Yeah that is it," Andy said. "It was nice. I was worried after I put the coffin down because I thought the priest was going to talk to me, and there was no way I would have been able to lipread him, the nose and hair was so distracting!"

"Well Marcia called me while you were being brought back," Miss Fleet said. "And I am amazed at the report she gave you."

"She offered me a job," Andy said.

"I know," Miss Fleet said in excitement. "That rarely happens, I mean, we had a student a few years ago who got offered a job in a supermarket, but never anything like this."

"It was a shock," Andy said.

"I take it you want to continue with your plans to study performing arts?" Miss Fleet said.

"Yes," Andy added. "I am planning to go to college to do performing arts. Applying next year."

"I admire you," Miss Fleet said. "Just remember that acting is a very overcrowded and hard profession, so have a think about it because opportunities like this don't always come along."

"I know," Andy nodded. "Thanks."

"Have you had lunch yet?" Miss Fleet asked.

"Yes," Andy said. "I am stuffed."

"Marcia said you refused money," Miss Fleet said. "Why?"

"It felt weird," Andy said.

Miss Fleet pulled an envelope from her bag and placed it in front of Andy.

"It's an undertaker's wages for a week," She said. "Gerald dropped them off after you walked into the building."

"Crafty sod," Andy said taking the wallet.

"You deserve it," She said. "They told me you worked hard all week, they were impressed with what you did in the coffin store and also the cold room, although that sounds creepy."

"I loved it," Andy said. "So much I am going to ask my local at home if I can spend some time with them in the holidays."

"Oh," Miss Fleet said. "Good for you, let me know if you want me to organise anything."

"I can sort it," Andy said. "Going to pop in there tomorrow and will give them Marcia's details if they need them."

"Plenty to write about?" Miss Fleet said. "Will you?"

"Already have been," Andy said. "Every evening I wrote for a while."

"Your housemother raised concerns," Miss Fleet said. "You are spending nearly all your time alone."

"I prefer it," Andy said. "People are idiots."

"Do you need to speak to me about anything?" Miss Fleet said. "Are you being bullied?"

"Did Terry tell you?" Andy asked.

"No," Miss Fleet said. "Clare is worried about you."

"I am fine," Andy said. "Nothing needs to happen."

"Okay," Miss Fleet nodded. "Can you do one thing for me though?"

"What?" Andy asked.

"Talk to someone," She said smiling. "Also another thing, I want to read about everything that happened in the last week."

"I can do that for you," Andy said. "You can then read about the idiot at the portering department."

"That reminds me," She said. "I had a call from a Sonja at the General, praising you and updating me on the issues with the portering role, so I apologise for that."

"It's okay," Andy said. "Everything happens for a reason."

"True," Miss Fleet said. "Very true."

"Can I go?" Andy asked. "I want to get out of this."

"Sure," She said. "Have a nice weekend and I look forward to seeing you at the beginning of the new term."

Andy smiled and left the room, closing the door and making his way towards the dorms. He pulled off the jacket, folding it and putting it under his arm.

Andy opened the door just as Terry was walking out.

"Hey Andy," Terry said. "You okay?"

"All good," Andy said.

"How was your last day?" Terry smiled. "Didn't steal any bodies I hope?"

"No," Andy laughed. "They wouldn't even let me take one."

Terry scoffed and shook his head.

"They did give me a week's salary though," Andy said. "Which was good of them."

"Well deserved," Terry said. "I look forward to reading about it."

"Andy!" someone called out. "That jacket is ugly!"

Andy turned around to see Ahmet walking up the path, wearing trainers, shorts, and a basketball t-shirt. His short black hair was thick with gel.

"Are you gay," He said. "Gay boy?"

"Stop it, Ahmet," Terry said. "Have some respect."

"I was asked to wear it for the mother," Andy said holding up the jacket."

"I wouldn't wear something lame like that!" Ahmet said.

"But would you do anything for anyone other than yourself?" Terry asked him. "No?"

"Whatever," Ahmet said. "Gay boy!"

"You are as funny as some of the bodies I dealt with this week," Andy said. "I am pretty sure I can arrange for you to be shoved in one and buried in the bloody sea!" Andy snapped.

"It's dirty working with the dead," Ahmet said. "My work experience was much more important."

"A sports shop?" Andy said. "Okay."

"Better than you," Ahmet said with a patronising grin on his face. Andy reached out.

"Touched dead people today," Andy said. "Shake my hand." Ahmet jumped back, putting his fists up and ready to fight.

"Grow up Ahmet," Terry said, getting in front of Andy. "You are not a street fighter."

"Watch your back!" Ahmet snapped.

"Stop threatening people," Terry said. "If I have one more complaint about you, I will make sure you spend next year in the year three dorm."

"You cannot do that," Ahmet said. "No way."

"I am the new dorm manager," Terry said. "I can make next year extremely uncomfortable for you, sharing a room with twenty other boys?"

"No way!" Ahmet said.

"Can you leave us please Ahmet," Terry said. "I am having a conversation with Andy."

"You gay too?" Ahmet said. "You want Andy to be your boyfriend?"

"Go away," Terry said. "Or next year you will not get your own room."

"Whatever!" Ahmet said, giving Andy the middle finger as he walked away."

Andy groaned, shaking his head.

"If he gives you any problems," Terry said. "You tell me. I'll put him in the cupboard downstairs if he keeps it up."

"He is a prick," Andy said. "And untouchable."

"Why do you say that?" Terry asked.

"Well his father is a millionaire Arab who gives the school money," Andy said. "Pricks like that get protected for life."

"Not quite," Terry said. "I have met his father, a nice guy and professional," He chuckled. "Pretty sure he would kick him to death if he knew what he gets up to at school."

"Oh right," Andy nodded knowingly.

"Also, might have to tell his dad his son likes bacon," Terry smiled.

Andy looked at him curiously.

"He is forbidden," Terry said. "Religious thing."

Andy nodded, shrugging his shoulders.

"I should have taken the job," Andy said.

"How come?" Terry said. "Changed your mind about acting?"

"No," Andy said. "At least I had access to a furnace for disposal of useless waste!"

Terry laughed as Andy walked past him and hit the stairs running.

"See you later!" Terry called out. "Think about it hard Andy, you would make a good undertaker, dark and creepy enough!" Terry laughed, pulling the door closed.

Printed in Great Britain
by Amazon